A Brief History of Biographies

A Brief History of Biographies
From Plutarch to Celebs

Andrew Brown

Brief Histories
Published by Hesperus Press Limited
19 Bulstrode Street, London WIU 2JN
www.hesperuspress.com

Designed and typeset by Fraser Muggeridge studio
Printed and bound by CPI Group (UK) Ltd, Croydon CRO 4YY

ISBN: 978-1-84391-972-8

Contents

Prologue
The Life of God

In 1996, a somewhat unusual biography was awarded a Pulitzer Prize. Its author had been a seminarian of the Society of Jesus (1960–70), an editor for various publications and presses (Doubleday, the University of California Press), held a Harvard PhD in Near Eastern Languages, and was a professor of humanities. His name was Jack Miles, and his book was called *God: a Biography*. This was not – as is ex-nun Karen Armstrong's *A History of God* (1993) – a narrative account of the way the concept of God has evolved; it was a 'life and works' study, showing how the life was revealed through the works, as recorded in the Jewish Bible, the *Tanakh*.

Miles's methodology shows an awareness of several centuries of what used to be called the 'Higher Criticism' and has now evolved into the set of academic disciplines that subject sacred scripture to critical analysis, drawing on philology, archaeology, history, papyrology, source analysis, sociology, and comparative religion – these days, in fact, a whole university of knowledge. But Miles also indulges in a deliberate and even wilful downplaying of this wealth of scholarly information in favour of a relatively 'straight' narrative reading of the *Tanakh*, based on the premise that it is the life story of a character known as 'God'. (Or 'G-d', or 'YHWH', or 'Yahweh', or 'Adonai', or 'the Name', etc.: 'God' will do as a misnomer.) Miles writes:

Can a literary character be said to live a life from birth to death or otherwise to undergo a development from beginning to end? Or is a literary character – fixed on the pages of a book, trapped forever in the same few words and actions – the very opposite of a living, developing human being?

Miles insists on the distinction between fictional and non-fictional 'character', but the very word 'character' straddles the divide. And his words raise a question about human beings as well as God. To what extent does the genre in which their tales are told give them a life that develops over time, or are they inevitably fixed on the page? How can their freedom (if they have any) be respected? Is 'essentialising' an unavoidable effect of the very nature of language, so that the distinction between real characters and fictional characters is invariably overridden in what is always, on one level, a linguistic artefact – more specifically, the literary genre known as biography?

I used to dislike biographies because they always began and (much worse) ended pretty much the same way. Miles is happy for his 'life' of God to have a beginning and an end:

If biography is seen narrowly as a branch of history, then there can be no biography of a nonhistorical character. But God does have a first and a last appearance in the Hebrew Bible. We see him first as the creator, outside history, prior to it, masterfully setting in motion the heavenly bodies by which historical time will be measured. We see him last as the 'Ancient of Days', white-haired and silent, looking forward to the end of history from a remote and cloudy throne. This book becomes a biography of a special sort by dint of its determination to describe the middle that lies between so vigorous a beginning and so quiescent an end.

Of course, this account is a biography of a doubly unusual kind in that we do not witness either the birth of God, or his death. The *Tanakh* takes God's existence as given (it rejects the theogonies of other religions of the Middle East: 'in the beginning' God is); and Nietzsche and his madman are not even dim surmises as the *Tanakh* draws to its end (God does not die in the last book of the *Tanakh*, Chronicles II, he only fades away).

Miles then describes in more detail the structure of this most peculiar biography:

The beginning and the end of the Hebrew Bible are not linked by a single, continuous narrative. Well short of the halfway point in the text, the narrative breaks off. What then follow are, first, speeches spoken by God; second, speeches spoken either to or, in some degree, about God; third, a protracted silence; and, last, a brief resumption of the narrative before a closing coda. The narrative suspense that lasts from the Book of Genesis through II Kings is succeeded, past that point, by another kind of suspense, one more like the kind jurors experience in a courtroom as different witnesses take the stand to talk about the same person. A sequence of testimonies – each in its own distinctive voice, with its own beginning and end – can be as effective as narrative in suggesting that the person about whom the words are spoken does not stop where the words stop. This is the biographical effect in another form. And even in this form, it is an effect that can include a sense of forward movement, of 'What next?'

The idea that a biography is essentially juridical (the judging of a life by the assembly of witnesses) is crucial, and we will meet it again. But in the trial of God known as the *Tanakh*, the defendant (who is also, of course, judge) has the right to silence. God's last words are those he speaks to Job out of the whirlwind. After that, he shuts up. (It is difficult to know quite what he could have followed *that* performance with.) Not only do his sayings end, the Bible speaks about him less and less. He is not even mentioned in the Book of Esther, in which his people, terrifyingly, are faced with the threat of utter extermination ('in effect, the Jews surmount the threat without his help,' observes Miles). God loves his people, and they love him, but at a distance. There is no longer the same hope-filled, querulous urgency of need and supplication as before; Israel's longing, impatience, resentment and backsliding, the whole dialectic of worship and revolt that had marked the earlier books, has been muted. God's 'stiffnecked' people have long since been chastised into submission and devoutness. There is a warm sunset haze, tinged with a frisson of anxiety and abandonment, in Miles's account of the last pages of the *Tanakh*. The life of what Nietzsche had admired as one of *the* great characters fades majestically away, as in some celestial retirement home, like a god on pension.

Miles's 'theography' stands in violent contrast with the God of the philosophers. The *concept* of God is that of a ground of being, outside time, immutable, unbounded. But such a concept, Miles points out, is found nowhere in the *Tanakh*, nor in the New Testament, where, in spite of (or, we might hazard, precisely because of, the ban on idolatry) the character of God is resolutely anthropomorphic: he seems – all too much to contemporary readers – snappy, over-hasty, arbitrary, vengeful, racist, misogynistic, and tribal (and not always in a good way). He is unpredictable, moody, sometimes spoiling for a fight, sometimes impossibly benign. For all the anthropomorphic imagery, God never settles down into a fixed personality, for almost all of his attributes are contradicted by their opposites, and they form a pattern which changes over time. Miles:

A strictly sequential reading of the Hebrew Bible is a way to recover the successiveness, the character development or theography, that 'Aristotelian' exegesis has obscured. Thus, Christians pray 'Our Father, who art in heaven...' as Christ did, and imagine that the being who says, at Genesis 1:3, 'Let there be light' is a father, but God does not refer to himself as a father at that point. Only several hundred pages later, in II Samuel 7, does he do this for the first time. Jews pray 'Blessed art thou, O Lord, our God, King of the Universe'; and imagine that the God of Genesis is a king, but he does not present himself as a king until even later, at Isaiah 6. 'Later' in this context does not mean later in historical time but simply later in the exposition, further along in a start-to-finish reading of the book. Historically speaking, the 'time' when God says 'Let there be light' lies outside time; but from the point of view of a reader beginning at the beginning of the Book of Genesis and reading straight on from there, we may still speak of 'later' and 'earlier'.

God's essence can doubtless be captured by a set of abstractions (those gabbled out by Lucky in *Godot*), but his existence is full of surprises. He is radically free: a scary prospect. He is freer, for example, than any character in Sartre (who tries, heroically, to trace every facet of Genet's life to an originary trauma, that of being labelled a 'thief').

How many subjects of 'traditional' biographies change in such a way? 'Little did young Bonaparte know, as he engaged in a snowball fight with his mocking schoolfellows in Ajaccio, that one day his genius for tactics would make him master of an empire that stretched', etc. Little do I know whether this event really took place; I simply remember it, rather vaguely, from Abel Gance's biopic. But the whole of Bonaparte is already latent in the proud, clever, resentful, provincial little boy in a way that the whole of God is not there in Genesis. It is said that the character of human beings is fixed when they are several months old. This alone excuses – to some extent – the purgatory of child-hood with which biographies traditionally begin. But it cannot be said of God. Actually, it is not really certain that it is true of human beings. Perhaps good biographies can provide some of the raw material for a proper philosophical discussion of this fraught question. But not even the best biographies can rival that which Miles so brilliantly finds written in the *Tanakh*.

There are lives of gods in other traditions: the many avatars of Siva or Krishna, for example. But they are a form of *lila* or play; manifestations of a life which transcends personality. In Hinduism, the gods and goddesses have many lives, so many that it becomes paradoxical to speak of them having biographies. The same applies to human beings, who are reincarnated from life to life. This insight was radicalised in Buddhism.

Part I
Religious Leaders and Saints

Lives of the Buddha

In the first watch of the night, as he sat in meditation under the *bodhidhruma* (Tree of Awakening) in the Deer Park of Varanasi, Gotama developed the power to remember his past lives. The 'Sutta on Fear and Trembling' (*Bhayabhereva Sutta*) in Pali states:

> When the mind was concentrated, purified, and cleansed, unblemished and free of defilements, malleable and workable, steady and undeflectable, I directed the mind to the knowledge of recollection of past places of birth. I recollected many different previous places of birth – one birth, two births, three births, four births, five births; ten births, twenty births, thirty births, forty births; a hundred births, a thousand births, a hundred thousand births; many aeons when [the universe] was contracting, many aeons when [the universe] was expanding – 'There I had such a name, such a family, such an appearance, such a diet; such was my experience of pleasure and pain, such my term of life; passing away from there, I arose elsewhere, and there I had such a name, such a family, such an appearance, such a diet; such was my experience of pleasure and pain, such my term of life; passing away from there I arose here' – In this manner I recalled different previous places of birth with their features and details.

This was the first cognition which I achieved in the first watch of the night. Ignorance was banished, and cognition arose; darkness was banished, and light arose, as happens for one who abides vigilant, ardent, and resolute.

The stories of the past lives of the Buddha, or *jatakas*, spread widely after his death. The *Devadhamma-Jataka* recounts one of these, in which the Buddha rebukes a wealthy, self-indulgent monk by revealing to him that, in a previous life, this monk had been a water-demon, while the Buddha himself had been a prince who showed the demon the meaning of true holiness – a lesson which, in his intervening incarnations, the wealthy monk had forgotten. And 'having told this story, the Master preached the Truths, and the Brother won the Fruit of the First Path'.

This story of a previous life of the Buddha forces us to envisage a world in which a biography stretches back countless aeons, through various forms (spirits, gods, demons, animals), each of which is determined by the previous life. Indeed, a biography is the strict unfolding of a transpersonal karma; there is not really any life story to be told because there is nobody whose life there is to tell. But it also shows how life (or lives) and doctrine are interchangeable, *even though* the doctrine transcends any one life. That is why the lives of the Buddha (including the stories about him that circulated during and after his last incarnation) are interwoven with his ideas, each spiralling round the other, as in a double helix. As Michael Carrithers has put it: 'As for his character apart from his philosophy, little can be said, for in our sources his character is his philosophy.' The Buddha himself knew that it was only within a life (apparently entrapped in biography) that life and biography were to be overcome. 'It is in this carcass, a fathom long, with its mind and its concepts, that I declare: there is the world; the origin of the world; the cessation of the world; and the path that leads to the cessation of the world.'

The *jatakas* are represented in many forms throughout the Buddhist world. They are engraved, for instance, on the walls of

Wat Si Chum, a temple complex outside Sukhothai in Thailand. Curiously, carved in dark corridors and up narrow stairwells, these beautiful 'lives of the Buddha' have always been difficult to access. It is almost as if they were meant to be hidden.

Life of the Dalai Lama

His eyes closed upwards like a bird's, and he had hands and feet webbed like a goose. He was a diligent ruler, but much less influential than his grandfather. He had extensions woven into his hair so that the members of the *sangha* could sit on his locks during discussions. His neck was broken by two of his ministers, perhaps while he was drinking *chang* (barley beer) in his garden. He mastered the art of Tibetan swift-footed running and, in six days, could cover distances that would usually require six months of travel. When he touched a rock, he left impressions of his hands and feet there. When he died, his body was transformed into that of a youth: it glowed with such radiance that few could bear to look on it. He bi-located, but his followers found this confusing, and the other monks frowned on such a practice. (On one occasion there were three of him.) He offered 1,000 Tibetan soldiers to help Britain in the First World War. Etcetera.

These deeds, which I have taken from Alexander Norman's *The Secret Lives of the Dalai Lama. Holder of the White Lotus* (2008), are all ascribed to the various incarnations of the Dalai Lama. There is a peculiar pungency to the 'lives' of Buddhists: every deed is illusory, every deed is absolutely crucial in the chain of karma.

More generally, what sense would a western-style biography have in radically different cultures (Kalahari bushmen, the shamans of Siberia, the Amazonian tribes studied by Lévi-Strauss in which the boundary between animal and human domains is so permeable, for example)?

Life of Jesus

Biopics are an interesting cinematic genre; some of the earliest films were biographies. We have looked at the *Tanakh* as a biography – some might say that the greatest of all biopics is also a 'life of God': the *Gospel According to Matthew*, by the Marxist and homosexual writer, poet and director Pier Paolo Pasolini. It is, like Miles's account, a biography at one remove, since its script relies almost verbatim on the biography attributed to Matthew.

What do we know of this Matthew? Apart from the fact that, in Hebrew, his name means 'gift of God', we have to piece his biography together from the Gospels (including his 'own'). He was born and brought up in Capharnaum (Kfar Nahum in Hebrew – 'Nathan's village'), a small but important town in Galilee (population in the reign of Herod the Great: some 1,500). Capharnaum was the birthplace of other people associated with the circle of Jesus of Nazareth, including Peter, Andrew, James and John – it may have been for this reason that Jesus made it the central base for his mission. Matthew (who is sometimes identified with Levi, since the latter is also called a 'son of Alpheus') was a tax collector – an agent of imperial domination, as he collected taxes from the Jews for the Romans (more specifically for the son of Herod the Great known as Herod Antipas, tetrarch of Galilee). He would have been viewed with resentment by his fellow Jews; despised as a political collaborator, an accomplice of idolaters, a near-heretic. His trade, balancing the books, would have required a degree of literacy, so he was probably fluent in Aramaic and Greek. He decided to abandon his dubious profession in favour of an even more dubious existence as the follower of an itinerant preacher, Jesus. (Jesus himself would have lost a degree of creditability among his fellow Jews by consorting with such a dodgy character as Matthew. He retorted, in his defiant way, that it was precisely 'sinners' such as tax collectors – even tax collectors! – that he was calling to repentance.)

Matthew duly became one of the Twelve; he was at the Last Supper, he witnessed the Crucifixion of Christ and his post-resurrection appearances; for fifteen years he preached the Gospel in Hebrew before (this is where tradition takes over) leaving Palestine for Macedonia, Persia, and Parthia. It is said that he was martyred; we do not know how.

Well before the end of the first century, orally transmitted stories about the life of Christ had been written down: one of the biographies compiled into a 'gospel', heavily reliant on earlier texts (Mark, 'Q', others that have been lost), was attributed to Matthew, this marginal figure with a shady past.

The life of Matthew consists essentially of one momentous event: his calling. It is this scene that is recorded again and again in art, most dramatically in the painting by Caravaggio (apparently homosexual, murderer, outlaw – all facts of relevance to our theme). His less well-known painting, *The Martyrdom of Saint Matthew*, in the church of San Luigi dei Francesi, Rome, was painted to a commission from his patron, the (probably bisexual – life ran very high in those days) Cardinal Francesco Maria del Monte. This painting is a whirlwind of light and darkness in which Matthew appears as a helpless old man sprawled on the steps of an altar while a muscular youth, naked apart from a loin cloth and a head band, grips his wrist and prepares to strike. It depicts the traditional story that Matthew had rebuked the king of Ethiopia for lusting after his own niece, and in punishment was slain by a soldier while saying Mass.

It is to the calling of Matthew that we owe these paintings (as well as the *St Matthew Passion* of J.S. Bach[1]). In *The Calling of Saint Matthew*, Christ, his figure largely concealed by (probably) another disciple, is swathed in darkness; the side of his face appears, swarthy, a little gaunt, intent; from the shadows emerges his right hand, pointing ambiguously at Matthew – the forefinger is extended, but its first two joints droop somewhat, and the other fingers, in the gloom, hang slackly, so that the gesture is both imperious and casual, accusing and inviting. Matthew's gesture is clearer, though not entirely so: he is (probably) pointing, left-handedly, to himself (at a spot on the right of his chest), but there is a hesitancy in the movement, and the hand as it emerges from the blackness of his garment might be aiming its question at the dark-haired youth bent in absorption over the coins on the table, and unaware of, or indifferent to, the two men who have just entered. (W.H. Auden might have written a poem about him.) Matthew may be saying, in mime, 'Do you mean me... or him?' Little does he know (this is a biographical prolepsis) that one day he will write the biography of the man who has suddenly turned up at his tax office, to look at him, point at him, and say 'Follow me' – or that, much later, also a result of this appearance, he will (perhaps) be killed, a bit ingloriously: no upside-down cross, like his friend Peter, or that other new variation on an ancient theme, the saltire version, like his other friend, Andrew – nothing that can be depicted with artistic brio or narrated in dramatic terms with clouds parting on high and cherubs making ready to receive him. Just bumped off in a *sale affaire*, somewhere a bit indeterminate, because an unnamed king fancied his own niece.

The death of Pier Paolo Pasolini nearly two millennia later remains almost equally mysterious. On 2 November 1975, on the beach at Ostia, the old harbour city of Rome, he was run over several times with his own car. Giuseppe Pelosi, a hustler, confessed to the murder. (Had Pasolini gone to the beach and met up with a bit of over-rough trade? This is an example of 'biographical speculation'.) Thirty years later, Pelosi retracted his confession; he had made it simply to protect his family, who had been threatened with violence. The real culprits, he claimed, had been three people who, in a southern Italian accent, jeered at Pasolini for being a 'filthy Communist'. Others have claimed that the murderer was an extortionist involved in the theft of several rolls of film of Pasolini's *Salò, or the 120 Days of Sodom*. (The police have since dropped the case for lack of new evidence.)

Pasolini had always been a controversial figure, intrigued by Catholicism and Communism, critical of both. After the Second World War, he moved to Rome and became familiar with the desperate living conditions of the urban proletariat in the city's *borgate*. He depicted these slum conditions in *Mamma Roma*, and celebrated urban life in *Accatone*. In 1963, he directed a short film, *La Ricotta*, that was one section of the four-part portmanteau production known as *Ro.Go.Pa.G.* (sometimes called 'Rogopag', the reference is to the four directors involved, one French and three Italian: Rossellini, Godard, Pasolini, and Gregoretti).

La Ricotta is set in a harsh hilly environment outside a city. A film director (played by Orson Welles but channelling some of Pasolini's own personality traits) is making a film of the Crucifixion. One of the bit players is a man from an impoverished family called *Stracci* ('Rags'). He has hardly anything to eat; what he does have, he gives to his wife and child. He dresses up in women's clothes and a wig in order to steal some food – but is called on to play his part (as 'the good thief') before he can eat it, and when he returns, his food has been devoured by a dog belonging to some of the wealthier film stars. By the time he eventually manages to buy some bread and cheese (the ricotta of the title), he is starving; he crams himself full. As a result, during the shoot, he dies of gastric congestion on the cross. The film was seen as blasphemous; Pasolini was charged with contempt for the state religion, under a fascist law that had not been rescinded (it was not the only one to have survived on the statute books of Italy), and sentenced to four years' imprisonment (the sentence was later quashed on appeal).

The Gospel According to Matthew came out in 1964 (Pasolini had begun work on it while shooting *La Ricotta*). Like all biographies, it needs to be seen in historical context. In January of that year, President Johnson declared a 'War on Poverty' and signed the Civil Rights Act; the space race intensified with the launching of Gemini 1; Nelson Mandela, at the opening of the Rivonia Trial, made his celebrated speech 'I am prepared to die'; the

Rolling Stones produced their first album; twelve men in New York City (which Pasolini loved – it was 'as beautiful as the Sahara desert') were the first to burn their draft cards in public, as a protest against the Vietnam War; and the Catholic Church condemned the oral contraceptive for women. There was a drastic food shortage in India.

The script for *The Gospel According to Matthew* was taken almost directly from the Gospel according to Matthew, in its resonant Italian translation that brought out the tenderness (the freckled angel of the Lord, to a startled, balding Joseph: '*Alzati, prendi con te il bambino e sua madre e fuggi in Egitto*' (Matthew 2:13)), the wrath of John the Baptist ('*Razza di vipere! [...] colui che viene dopo di me [...] brucerà la pula con un fuoco inestinguibile*' (Matthew 2:7–12)), and Christ's fierce denunciations of the learned of his day ('*Guai a voi, scribi e farisaei ippocriti!*' (Matthew 23:23)). Some biographies just work better in certain languages. (The role of Mary at the foot of the cross, incidentally, was played, with beautiful *verismo*, by Pasolini's mother Susanna.)

Why did Pasolini choose Matthew over the other evangelists? His reply was crisply worded: 'John was too mystical, Mark too vulgar, and Luke too sentimental.' New Testament scholars have sometimes concurred with this judgement, albeit in more nuanced tones. John's biography of Jesus does indeed begin in other-worldy tones, with a recapitulation of the beginning of Genesis, but couched in terms as close to Stoic and neo-Platonic philosophy (the Logos) as they are to the Jewish theology of creation; his Jesus moves in a world charged with symbol and metaphor, and the style of his discourses reaches a climax in the Last Supper ('I am the vine, ye are the branches'). Mark, often seen as the earliest gospel to be redacted, is written in a relatively plain and homely (though 'vulgar' is an exaggeration) version of *koine* Greek (and it notoriously ends, in the best manuscripts, not with the resurrection appearances but with an enigmatic frisson of suspense, some women running away from the empty tomb, saying nothing to anybody, 'for they were afraid'). And the holy, glorious and all-laudable Apostle and evangelist Luke was a doctor (and also, according to the traditions, an artist – we have three portraits by him of the Blessed Virgin and her son, albeit in three quite different styles: one is in Poland – the haunting Black Madonna of Cz stochowa; one is in the monasteries of Hodegon and Soumela in Istanbul, and Our Lady of Vladimir is now in Moscow).[2] Luke's account of the Nativity is the fullest, as one would expect from a physician: he shows an unusual interest in Mary and more generally in the female followers of Jesus; he is full of compassion for the suffering, ready to extend the good news to gentiles; he has kind words even for the outcast and the despised (in Luke's gospel alone do we find the parables of the Good Samaritan and the Prodigal Son). Perhaps his biography *is* prone to a certain lyricism, but Pasolini's charge of sentimentality is a tad severe. Still, one can understand why he chose the altogether tougher Matthew: more Jewish than Greek, with a vein of violence and apocalypticism – his gospel contains the discourses on the Last Judgment, it constantly divides the world into sheep and goats, and it has an urgency, a clarity, and a prophetic fury to it that lend themselves readily to the screen.

In the film, Jesus was played by the nineteen-year-old Enrique Irazoqui, in a performance of overwhelming *charisma* (this word, a cliché in the performing arts, is for once unusually apt). Irazoqui appeared in three later, far less celebrated films, but has mainly made a name for himself as an economist (he claimed that he had read Marx, but learned nothing about accounting from him), as a professor of literature, and as an expert on chess, especially computer chess. Long before Deep Blue inflicted its wound on human vanity, Irazoqui played against Marcel Duchamp; against Marcel's wife, Teeny Duchamp (who took her defeats much less badly than her competitive and perfectionist husband); and against John Cage, the celebrant of chance. As a member of a clandestine trade union in Franco's Spain, Irazoqui (whose mother was Italian, so he spoke the language) was sent, at the age of nineteen, to Italy to make contact with fellow left-wingers.

He gave a speech in the house of a poet in Rome; Pasolini approached him afterwards and offered to go to Spain to help the cause, in return for just one favour: he wanted Irazoqui to play Christ on screen. He had long been looking for a suitably Christ-like figure, he said, but so far in vain. Irazoqui retorted that he had better things to do. Why waste his time in the service of a reactionary ideology that still held his county in the chains of a military-clerical dictatorship? He was more interested in establishing 'human fraternity'. In the end, only the advocacy of the writer Elsa Morante (she would later break off her friendship with Pasolini when he wrote a critical review of the political short-comings of her novel *History*)[3] persuaded Irazoqui to take on the part. Filming in Calabria was unsettling: lots of men in black suits asked him to perform miracles; they were aghast at the fact that (when not filming) he smoked, and behaved like an ordinary mortal – just like one of them, in fact. On his return to Spain, the police confiscated his passport for appearing in 'a Marxist film'.

One feature that differentiates Matthew's gospel from the other three is the genealogy with which it begins; all the 'begats' that initially seem a rather dull way to begin a biography that is to be filled with such drama and passion. (It sounds better when solemnly chanted, as at the beginning of the Mass by Monteverdi, first performed in San Marco, Venice, on 21 November 1631 to celebrate Venice's deliverance from the plague, rising to the triumphant acclamation '*qui vocatur Christus*'.) In a sermon on 'The genealogy of Christ', Herbert McCabe OP once read out these first seventeen verses. Then he put some flesh and blood on it – 'and there is a good deal both of the flesh and of blood involved'. Matthew is more down to earth than John or Luke – this genealogy shows how 'Jesus really was tied into the squalid realities of human life and sex and politics'. McCabe notes the numerical pattern that has dictated this genealogy (seven is a significant number for Matthew: there are twice seven generations from Abraham to David; another fourteen from David until the exile; and fourteen more from the exile until the coming of Christ). McCabe ignores the question of whether some editor has here tampered with history (history is such an inventive editor anyway), and focuses on the unhappy family history that lies behind the good news. Abraham nearly cut his son's throat; Jacob was a liar and a cheat; Judah had sex with his daughter-in-law Tamar, who had dressed up as a prostitute, and almost had her burned alive – and so on, via idolaters, fornicators and murderers. 'The moral is too obvious to labour: Jesus did not belong […] to the honest, reasonable, sincere world of the *Observer* [sic] or the *Irish Times*, he belonged to a family of murderers, cheats, cowards, adulterers and liars.'

Many other biographies – in pages that hasty readers tend to skip – begin with an account of their protagonist's ancestors, the human mulch in which their hero is rooted; but few have such an eccentric and alarming back story as that provided by Matthew for his own hero.

Jesus' life, too, accrued many myths, was told in many different ways. The Gnostic gospels often focused on his otherwise mysterious childhood. Playing with other children, he slides down a rainbow, and invites his playmates to do the same. They break their necks.

Another life of Jesus includes many unfamiliar features. He was in fact a bastard, born to Miriam when her fiancé, a nobleman by the name of Yochanan, of the line of David, was away, and she was raped by Yosef ben Pandera, possibly a Roman soldier also known as Pantera. Even worse, she was menstruating at the time, and thus ritually impure. When Jesus was a boy, he scandalised the sages by appearing bareheaded before them. Jesus' miracles were the results of sorcery. He even penetrated the Temple and learned the sacred name of God, which cannot be spoken; he then made a bird of clay, uttered the Name, and with it made the bird fly. He scandalised the Jews with another assault on the Temple and was hanged on a cabbage stalk, since his magic powers enabled him to break any tree. He was buried, but his disciples stole his body and pretended that he had risen from the dead.

These stories are told in the *Toledot Yeshu*, the 'History of Jesus'. They adopt a Jewish perspective and may have started circulating in the fourth century AD; they were certainly current in the Middle Ages. They are best seen as a Jewish response to intense Christian persecution: some of the stories, especially those of those of Jesus' miracles which resemble pointless conjuring tricks, are very like those which Christians invented to defame Simon Magus, and, later, Mohammed. (Most religions have concocted counter-biographies of the founders of rival religions.) What may have arisen as a cry of despair and resentment among a harshly persecuted people was inevitably turned against them. Christians decided that these were the fables which the Jews put about to slander Christ. This is biography as the site of a religious agon, a power struggle, a strategy of communal survival.

It was Oscar Wilde who wrote: 'Every great man has his disciples, and it is always Judas who writes the biography.' This is a little unfair on Matthew, Mark, Luke, and John, not to mention Jack Miles *et al*. But there is an additional twist in the fact that we do indeed possess the *Gospel of Judas*, published recently, and adding a great deal to our knowledge of the subject.

So much, then, for the greatest story ever told (the title of the remarkable 1965 film starring the intensely blue-eyed Max von Sydow (Jesus), Charlton Heston (John the Baptist), an alluring Carroll Baker (Veronica), David McCallum (Judas), and a brief cameo by John Wayne (the Centurion). See also *Jesus of Nazareth*, *The Passion of the Christ*, *Jesus of Montreal*, *La Vie de Jésus*, etc. Can they all, really, be 'lives of Jesus'?

Life of Mohammed

On the seventeenth night of Ramadan, an angel came to Mohammed and said: *iqra!* – 'recite!' This is how it all started: an act of dictation that was so unprecedented, so terrifying, that the Prophet at first thought that he was possessed by a *jinni*.

Biographers have struggled ever since to imagine what such an experience must have been like.

Although in many ways the Koran is the book that super-seded all other books, it has in fact been supplemented by the hadith. These are the words of the Prophet Mohammed, and they are essential aspects of his biography. As with Jesus, the life – not just the words, but the deeds – of the founder, or revealer, of a religion have binding force on the behaviour of believers. Since the prescriptions of the Koran often appear general, their application in specific cases is helped by reference to what the Prophet may have said or done on specific instances during his life.[4] Is it possible to lend items? One hadith (the Mu'jam al-saghir of al-Tabarani) states: 'The Messenger of God bought a camel from me; he then allowed me to ride it back to the city.' So it seems that it is permissible to lend items, since the Prophet did.

These hadith were remembered by those who had known the Prophet (especially his close friends and supporters, those known as the Companions of the Prophet) and eventually recorded; the first such collection is the *Muwatta* of Malik ibn Anas. They were inscribed in notebooks of papyrus, on parchment, or even on palm fronds; they were often prefaced by the formula: 'the Prophet of God said...' Aisha, one of Mohammed's wives, was an especially valuable source for more personal details of the Prophet's domestic life (and women played a significant part in transmitting the sayings across the generations – Karima al-Marwaziyya being an important example). The hadith capture the Prophet's charismatic author-ity: they are essentially lapidary. Mohammed did not view himself as the author of the Koran; he was merely the vessel for God's revelation, not a word of which could be altered. It was seen as permissible, however, to paraphrase some of the Prophet's sayings – and, since his deeds were recorded by the Companions, the words used were theirs (a form of biograph-ical attribution: he said this, he did that). This was largely an oral culture, words would be memorised and passed on by word of mouth. Only when discrepancies in memory started to become an issue, and after the death of the Prophet, did Muslims resort to writing: in the case of the hadith, 'biophonemes' became, as it were, 'biographemes' (as was also the case with the Buddha and Jesus).

Reports on the Prophet could sometimes contradict one another, and Islam was soon involved in fierce doctrinal debates. The temptation to put a spin on the Prophet's words, or even to invent sayings that would accord with one's own ideological stance, was not always resisted. Forged hadith started to appear. It was claimed, for instance, that Mohammed had declared: 'The people with the greatest destiny in Islam are the people of Persia' – a hadith that played a prominent role in works composed in Nishapur and Isfahan, those great Persian cultural centres. In response, a form of stringent textual analysis arose, designed to check the authenticity of the sayings. The word 'isnad' (meaning 'support') was used to refer to the chain of transmitters through whom the text (matn) could be traced back to the Prophet himself. Something of the tension between oral and written language persisted; the idea of a long line of human bodies going back to Mohammed helped to give flesh to the words they passed on, since reading a book without receiving it from a teacher was like 'trying to light a lamp without any oil'. But flesh is erring, and it was seen as essential to scrutinise the texts as well as the credibility of their mortal vehicles. Mohammed himself had warned against attributing false words or deeds to him: 'If anyone lies about me deliberately [this word was missing in some accounts], he should prepare for himself a seat in Hellfire.' Still, even hadith that were deemed unreliable could be influential. 'If anyone memorises, on behalf of my community, forty hadiths from my Sunna, I will be his intercessor on the Day of Judgment' was one saying that provided a stimulus to the learning and passing on of collections of the hadith. The Prophet's life on earth had ended, but he was still actively guiding his followers. So he appeared, in a dream, to Jalal al-Di al-Suyuti (d. 1505), saying, 'Bring forth the Sunna! Bring forth the hadith!' – spurring on the production of the Jam' al-jawami' or *Consolidation of Compendia*.

Although the distinction between the revealed Koran and the biography of the Prophet is crucial, Mohammed's life was inevitably changed by the book dictated to him. At crucial junctures in his life, he would quote the Koran: the scripture of which his life was a vehicle inspired the decisions he made in that life, which in turn inspired the hadith, which in turn inspire believers. One of the Quraysh leaders, Utbah ibn Rabiah, dangled the promise of money and power before the Prophet's eyes. (The topos of 'temptation resisted' is an essential one in the biographies of founders of religions.) Mohammed riposted by quoting the Koran, 41:1–10, and continued up to verse 38. Then he prostrated himself. Utbah was convinced: he returned to the Quraysh (but his pleas to them to abandon their hostility to the Prophet remained unheeded).

During the *hijrah*, the flight to Medina, Mohammed was forced to hide for a while in a cave (*ghar Thawr*), with the Quyraysh in pursuit. Some of them spotted the cave in which he and his followers had taken refuge. Abu Bakr saw them, but Mohammed whispered to him, 'Do not be afraid for God is with us.' He also said: 'What do you think of this [people] whose third is God?' The first of these reassuring sayings is a quotation from the Koran (9:40); the second is a hadith of al-Bukhari. The men of Quraysh saw a spider's web that had been woven over the mouth of the cave, and noticed that a dove had built its nest there. Clearly, nobody had entered this cave recently: they left without exploring it further.

Mohammed continued on his way to Medina. If I have understood the tradition properly, his was a life constructed under the unimaginable pressure of its being the *sole* medium through which was revealed a message that infinitely transcended him.

Lives of the Saints

For ye are dead, and your life is hid with Christ in God

The Apostolic Constitution *Divinus perfectionis magister*, issued by John Paul,[5] Bishop, Servant of the Servants of God, for posterity, given in Rome, at Saint Peter's, on the 25th day of the month of January in the year 1983, the fifth of his pontificate, declared:

> At all times, God chooses [...] many who, following more closely the example of Christ, give outstanding testimony to the Kingdom of heaven by shedding their blood or by the heroic practice of virtues. The Church, in turn, from the earliest beginnings of Christianity has always believed that the Apostles and Martyrs are more closely joined to us in Christ and has venerated them, together with the Blessed Virgin Mary and the holy Angels, with special devotion, devoutly imploring the aid of their intercession. To these were soon added others also who had imitated more closely the virginity and poverty of Christ and, finally, others whose outstanding practice of the Christian virtues and whose divine charisms commended them to the pious devotion of, and imitation by, the faithful. [...]
>
> [The Church] proposes to the faithful for their imitation, veneration and invocation, men and women who are outstanding in the splendour of charity and other evangelical virtues and, after due investigations, she declares them, in the solemn act of canonisation, to be Saints.

But, like Jack Miles, Wojtyla had read the Higher Criticism; he was perfectly well aware that the machinery that had manufactured saints over the centuries was becoming a little rusty. Noting that 'recent progress in the field of historical studies has shown the necessity of providing the competent Congregation with an apparatus better suited for its task so as to respond more adequately to the dictates of historical criticism, Our Predecessor of happy memory, Pius XI' had set up a Historical Section to submit claims to sainthood to a more stringent examination. *Divinus perfectionis magister* set out the new norms: the role of bishops in enquiring about 'the life, virtues or martyrdom and reputation of sanctity or martyrdom, alleged miracles, as well as, if it be the case, the ancient cult of the Servant of God, whose canonisation is sought'. ('Servant of God' is a useful term: you cannot suggest yourself as a candidate for sainthood, so you are not a candidate for a post; and those who are potentially to be acknowledged as saints are not 'potential saints', or 'saints in waiting', since when the Church officially labels them as 'saints', it is recognising that something is already true.)

The Bishop was to seek out 'accurate information' about the life of the Servant of God and to ensure that any writings that he or she had left were 'examined by theological censors'. If these were found to 'contain nothing contrary to faith and good morals, then the Bishop should order persons qualified for this task to collect other unpublished writings (letters, diaries, etc.) as well as all documents, which in any way pertain to the cause. After they have faithfully completed their task, they are to write a report on their investigations.' Witnesses were also to be summoned and interviewed. The bishops were to behave, in other words, like professional biographers, with the slight difference that further investigations focused on the particular 'virtues or martyrdom' of their subjects, with a separate enquiry into 'alleged miracles'. For these reasons, an essential aspect of acclaiming someone as a saint is the writing of their biography – though this is preparatory to even more detailed investigations into the Servant's life by a 'postulator'. The 'heroic virtue' expected of a saint involves the three cardinal virtues (faith, hope and charity) and the four cardinal virtues (prudence, justice, fortitude and temperance); a bright array of these will make you 'venerable' and 'heroic in virtue'. Also, a declaration of '*non cultus'* must be made; in other words, it must be demonstrated that no improper cult, no superstitious or heretical worship has sprung up around the candidate's tomb.[6] The Servant's body is to be exhumed and examined, and relics are taken.

One of the features of the process of canonisation as it had hitherto existed was rationalised out of existence in Wojtyla's reform. This was the office of the *Promotor fidei*, the 'Promoter of the Faith' (more popularly known as the Devil's advocate), charged with uncovering any traces of unsaintly behaviour in the life of the Servant. Now that the Devil is no longer formally represented at these processes, there is no brake on the creation of new saints, which has accelerated dramatically. Wojtyla was being hailed as 'Santo Subito' before he was even in his grave.

Life of Rancé

The writing of biographies can sometimes be a penitential task. (So can reading them.) The ageing Chateaubriand was instructed by his confessor to write a biography, not of a saint, but of an equally inspiring figure: Rancé, the founder of the Trappists. Chateaubriand set about his task with reluctance. But his biography (the last work he wrote) shows considerable fascination for the way a young man about court, who enjoyed hunting, gambling, food, and sex (he was an ordained priest), decided to take up the most austere of vocations. One impetus may have been the discovery that his mistress had died, and – when he arrived at the scene – her head severed from the trunk, either because the body was too long to fit into the coffin, or for some anatomical investigation to be performed, or for some other reason. The story is unclear; Chateaubriand elides it in a haze of equivocation and conjecture. But his work, a superb rhetorical performance, confronts, though it cannot mimic, Rancé's silence; the silence enjoined on all Trappists. These Cistercians of the Strict Observance have no life outside that scripted for them. How can one write their biographies once they have joined the Order? (Rancé himself composed the *Lives of the Solitaries* – even more of a 'limit-text' than Chateaubriand's.)

In 1864, Richard Wagner had already composed *Tannhäuser*, *Lohengrin*, *Tristan und Isolde*, and *Die Meistersinger*, and was deep into the composition of the *Ring*. In the same year, Ludwig II became king of Bavaria and summoned Wagner to Munich. He paid off the composer's debts, and committed himself to staging Wagner's huge operas. Wagner's professional future seemed more assured than at any time previously. At the king's behest, he started to dictate his autobiography (*Mein Leben*). In this year, he also read Chateaubriand's *Life of Rancé*.

Life of St Agnes

Zola's novel *The Dream* tells of how, in the winter of 1860, the River Oise freezes over. A nine-year-old girl has taken refuge under the archway of the portal of St Agnes in the cathedral of Beaumont. Overcome with cold and exhaustion, she has been leaning against the central pier of the portal, with its statue of St Agnes, 'the thirteen-year-old martyr, a young girl just like her, holding her palm, and with a lamb at her feet'. Zola tells us more about this saint: the tympanum depicts the legend, a virgin child betrothed to Jesus who rejects the governor's son and is sent to work in a brothel as punishment – but her hair grows long enough to clothe her body. She is burnt at the stake but the flames part miraculously to spare her, while consuming her executioners. Her bones perform miracles, and even a painted statue of her gives peace to the priest Paulinus when he is wracked by the temptations of the flesh.

The young girl, Angélique, is found and taken in by a kindly, childless couple, Hubert and Hubertine, makers of ecclesiastical vestments. She reaches the age of twelve, the age of first communion, when restlessness sets in. She is rummaging around Hubert's workshop one day when she finds a very ancient in-quarto copy of *The Golden Legend*, by Jacopo da Varazze (usually Latinised as Jacobus de Voragine), bound in yellow calfskin, translated from the Latin in 1549.

Jacobus (c. 1230–98) was an Italian Dominican friar. His *Golden Legend* was filled with information on church matters, but was mostly celebrated for the lives of the saints which it contained. As Zola suggests, it was part of the equipment of a chasuble-maker, who needed to know the stories of the saints, their emblems, and the tools of their martyrdom that so often figured in the vestments he made. Angélique is transfixed, first by the engravings in the book, with their decorated letters: St John the Almsgiver is handing out money to the poor; St Mathias is smashing an idol; St Nicholas in his bishop's robes is standing near the little boys in a tub whom he resurrected after they had been killed and salted down by a butcher. From the images, Angélique progresses to the words, though she is frightened by the 'two serried columns of text, printed in an ink that was still deep black on the yellowed paper', and its 'barbaric' Gothic type. But she perseveres, manages to decode the abbreviations and read the old French, and is soon rapt into another world by the biographies of the saints recorded by Jacobus: 'The *Legend* fired her with such passion that she remained bent over it, her head in her hands, totally absorbed, eventually leaving her everyday life far behind, losing all sense of time, and gazing on as, from the depths of the unknown, the great dream unfolded.' It is a leitmotif of the book that, for a young woman of her upbringing and character, natural and supernatural are part of a continuum – or each one is the 'dream' of the other. Zola presents us with a mosaic of quotations and paraphrases, the kind of enthralled jumble of hagiographic detail that Angélique assembles from her reading. The saints may be prophets or martyrs, bishops or monks, virgins or whores, royal or beggarly in class; but they are all saints. 'They all have the same life story; they grow up for Christ, believe in him, refuse to sacrifice to false gods, are tortured and die in glory.' They can kill dragons, raise and calm tempests, and hover two cubits above the ground. (When Angélique makes her first communion, she has the same, albeit more metaphorical, sense of levitation.)

Every saint – like Jesus – has to confront devils: 'They flee aboute us as flyes, they fylle the air without nombre. [...] This ayer is also full of devylles & of wicked spyrytes as the sonne beme is full of small motes whiche is small dust or powder.'[7] Every hagiography details encounters with these malevolent spirits, in which they must be fought off by the saint. Fortunatus exorcises a woman of 6,666 of them; Basil goes *mano a mano* with them; Macarius spends a whole night in a graveyard trying to keep them at bay. Satan himself assails many of the saints: he can disguise himself as a woman, he can disguise himself as a saint. (The corollary of this, which Zola leaves implicit here, is that many a person who appears saintly may be the Devil in disguise – something which the Catholic clergy know from experience. And, more generally, a biographer who indulges in hagiography may be pandering to diabolical forces.) But if you can face down the Devil, he will appear as he hideously is: 'A blacke cat, bigger than a dogge, its eyes huge and flaumynge, its tongue hangynge down to the navel all broade and bloodye, the tayle twisted and raysed uppe showing its arse from whence there did yssue forth a greate and stinking smel.'

Angélique is fourteen and pubescent when she becomes captivated by the lives of the saints. 'When she read the *Legend*, her ears buzzed, and the blood thrummed in the little blue veins of her temples; and now she started to feel an affectionate kinship with virgins', especially Agnes, under whose statue she was found amid the virgin snow. Agnes is a good patron saint: her name was linked to the Greek *hagnos* (holy), the Latin *agnus* (lamb: pure and meek), and, more tangentially, the Latin *agnoscere* (to know, as in 'to know the way'). Here is Agnes repelling the advances of the governor's son as she comes out of school: 'Go fro me thou fardell of synne, nourysshynge of evylles & morsel of death, and departe.' How much sweeter is the love of the heavenly bridegroom!

> I am now embraced of hym of whom the mother is a vyrgyn. And his fader knewe never woman to whom the aungelles doo serve, the sonne & the mone mervayle them of his beaute whoswe werkes never fayle [...] by whose odoure dead men ryse agen to lyfe.

She eventually falls in love with Félicien, the son – from his pre-priestly life – of the Bishop of Beaumont (who has arranged for Félicien to marry an aristocrat, Mademoiselle Claire de Voincourt). But Angélique paradoxically imagines that a marriage which transgresses the boundaries of class can be arranged 'with the ease of the miracles in the *Legend*'. But her saints cannot help her to live; only to die. Just after her marriage to Félicien, in a splendid nuptial mass in the cathedral of Beaumont, she simply fades away, in a white-out of transcendence that takes her back to the virgin snow from which she had first emerged.

It is always difficult to *depict* sanctity. In some ways, even when expressed in works of charity, and despite the sometimes spectacular signs by which it is accompanied (Saint Teresa's levitations, which she seems to have viewed as a bit of a bore), it is a minimal form of life. In Gide's *Strait is the Gate*, the young woman, Alissa, who is tempted by sainthood dies away from life: she is in love with her cousin Jérôme, but wills this love (and thus herself) out of existence. She is an intelligent, articulate woman, but the entries in her diary become ever shorter; they eventually consist of quotations from the Scriptures interspersed with cries of anguish. Language cannot signify sainthood; this crisis in communication allies Alissa with some of her contemporaries who, as writers and artists, questioned all forms of representation (Malevich, 'White on White'; Mallarmé, the poetics of gaps and swerves; Webern, for whom, at one point, once the musical motif had been stated, there was nothing more to say – not much material for the garrulities of a biography here). Alissa is perhaps not a saint, but she is the next best thing, a modernist.

In biopics, of course, the problem of representing the lives of the 'holy', or the inner struggles of those who try to be so, is compounded. *Of Gods and Men* was an interesting recent attempt: as the monks tussle with the temptation to flee, their Father Superior tells one of the waverers, 'you died when you entered the Order'. There is something immensely consoling about this: if you are already dead, your biography is complete. Like a Jesuit, you obey, *perinde ac cadaver*. (Of course, every Christian, on baptism, *dies*.) No more biography! What a relief! Or rather: pure biography, with no autobiography (no autonomy); your life is part of something bigger than you. But *Of Gods and Men* is a film, and, however moving it may be, it rejoices in the impurity of film. The marvellous grizzled old doctor-monk is played by Michel Lonsdale. One of his earlier roles, when he was less grizzled, was as 'the hatter' in Bunuel's *The Phantom of Liberty*, in which he appeared wearing trousers without a seat, allowing his bare bottom to be lashed by a leather-clad dominatrix. Lambert Wilson, who plays the Superior, Christian, was once the face of Calvin Klein, starring notably in a poster ad for their fragrance aptly named 'Eternity' in 1998. This whiff of profanity at least helps to remove any suspicion of squeaky-clean sanctimoniousness in *Of Gods and Men*. The saint, one of the most authentic forms of being imaginable, is *also* a role (which merely heightens its authenticity).

Life of Gemma Galgani

The life of *Blessed Gemma Galgani* (1878–1903), by Father Amedeo, C.P., translated from the Italian by Father Osmund Thorpe, C.P., was published in London in 1935 by Burns, Oates & Washbourne, publishers to the Holy See.[8] As such, the biography had to be granted the 'Nihil obstat' and the 'Imprimatur' by British Catholic authorities. The first guaranteed that the book 'contains nothing contrary to faith or morals', while the second is the final statement that it 'may be published', even though those who permit publication may not agree with its contents. The book was a Passionist endeavour: 'C.P.' stands for 'Congregation of the Passion (of Our Lord Jesus Christ)', a congregation (similar to a religious order) founded by Saint Paul of the Cross in 1725 to promote missionary work and contemplation. The translator, a Passionist, says that he has followed the Italian text closely. There is a foreword by the then Catholic Archbishop of Liverpool, Richard Downey, which sets the text in its historical context. He writes:

> The publication is timely, as the cause of her canonisation is in hand, and her life contains many lessons which are particularly applicable to modern conditions. It is a little startling to realize that were she alive to-day she would be only fifty-seven years of age. She is then a modern, a contemporary of many living men and women, a person who in our times led a life of extraordinary sanctity. [...] In twenty-five years she scaled the ladder of perfection and left us a pattern of conformity in all things to the will of God.

Finally, we read: 'In obedience to the decrees of Urban VIII, and to the Apostolic Constitution "Officiorum" of Leo XIII, we declare that we claim no authority for what is written in this book other than that which is purely human and historical.'

Human and historical – there could be no better pair of epithets for what we expect from a biography. The other paraphernalia surround the life we are about to read (which duly starts with Gemma's birth: 'A day of rejoicing occurred on March 12, 1878, in the home of the chemist of Camigliano, a smiling village at the foot of the blue Pizzorne near Lucca in Italy. Another child had come to gladden the hearts of Enrico Galgani and Aurelia Landi, who already had three children'), with the panoply of Catholic authority and ritual declarations of doctrinal correctness (or at least inoffensiveness), with a clear statement about why this biography is worth publishing, and why *now* (Gemma is a role model, she has already been beatified and may soon be pronounced a saint). A startling, haunting photograph of Gemma stands before all these words as a frontispiece: dressed sombrely, her collar buttoned up, with her hair neatly combed over a broad forehead, a rectilinear, almost cubist-looking nose, a hint of sensuality in the nostrils, and a slight smile, she gazes out at the reader; a modern girl, perhaps a bit withdrawn. Other photographs conform more to the Saint-Sulpicien tampering so prevalent in traditional iconography: she poses, or is posed, gazing upwards, or her photograph is colourised into cheap images. Curiously, the photogenicity of sainthood comes across in a remark made by her uncle who, observing her at prayer when she was about four, said, 'If I had a camera I would have taken her photograph!' Gemma's photographs are inseparable from her biography.[9]

The titles and subtitles of the chapters indicate Gemma's[10] far from easy path to sanctity, from 'Birth and Early Years', via, '"I will strive to be a saint"', 'A model pupil', 'Give me Jesus!', 'A year of desolation', 'A severe judge of herself', 'Heroic resolutions', and so on, to 'Her triumph', which tells of her beatification on 14 May 1933. Father Amedeo's work can draw on Gemma's own *Autobiographia* (which she thought of as 'the book of her sins'), on an earlier biography by her confessor, the Passionist Fr Germanus of St Stanislaus, and on eyewitness accounts, including those gathered in the *Summarium Proc. super virtutibus*, the volume devoted to Gemma's virtues that was prepared during the processes for her beatification. This *Summarium* at times reads, as one might expect such documents to read, like a school report. Here is the *satisfecit* it awarded Gemma's family: 'The Galgani family occupied a good position in society, bore an exemplary character, and was most exact in the fulfilment of its religious duties.'

Father Amedeo's biography draws many parallels between Gemma's life and those of other saintly women (Thérèse of Liseux, Blessed Bartolomea Capitano).[11] There were shadows, too, on her young life. We learn that Gemma did not like being touched, even by her beloved father ('Early Growth in Holiness'). She had to watch as her mother Aurelia slowly died of tuberculosis. She was looking forward to wearing her gold medal for catechism, a gold pendant given her by her father, a gold watch; but then she saw her guardian angel looking at her, telling her that 'the ornaments of a spouse of a Crucified King are thorns and the Cross'. She suffered what in the biographies of mystics is called 'the dark night of the soul'. Her beloved brother Gino died, also of tuberculosis, and she herself was diagnosed with caries in a bone of her foot. Her father died, the creditors pounced (the family had fallen on hard times), and she went to live with her aunt and uncle. On hearing of her father's death (at which she was not present), she cried: 'Now it is time for me to be a nun.' But ill health supervened: she suffered increasingly from curvature and then tuberculosis of the spine, and was soon comparing this to crucifixion. She borrowed, and read, the *Life of Confrater Gabriel*, a Passionist. When she had to return it, she wept, but St Gabriel appeared to her that night in a dream to console her. This was the first of the 'ecstasies, visions, raptures, apparitions of angels, saints, the Blessed Virgin, and even of Christ Himself' that were to dominate Gemma's life from now on, says Fr Amedeo. Curious: a biography – but one that she has to 'sacrifice' – gives her contact with a new, supernatural world. Meanwhile, doctors applied the cauterising irons to her spine, and a tumour was discovered on her head; she seemed to be dying, in great pain, and on 2 February 1899 was given the *viaticum*. But she was advised to make a novena to St Margaret Mary Alacoque, and through a haze of pain did so: she was vouchsafed more visions; then she was cured.

Her desire to be a nun had become ever more pressing, but she was refused entrance to the Passionist Congregation, partly because of her ill health, partly because of her visions, which even in the most pious communities aroused misgivings. The doors of the Convent of the Visitation were closed against her. She started to mortify herself more severely, with a hairshirt and a knotted cord. On the Feast of the Sacred Heart, 1899, she had another vision of Jesus with his wounds open, but this time, fire rather than blood flowed from them, and touched her hands, feet and heart. She swooned; and when she came round, she was bleeding in those places. She had received the stigmata. From then on, from her head, her hands, and her feet, she would bleed, regularly and copiously.

Stigmatics can be men or women: St Francis of Assisi and, more recently, Padre Pio, are famous male cases. There is an odd sexualisation in the process of being pierced, however. Father Amedeo here comments: 'Her ardent desire [to share in Christ's suffering] is now satisfied. In her virginal flesh she bears the wounds of her Divine Spouse. Now she can say with St. Paul the Apostle: "I bear in my body the marks of the Lord Jesus".' This is a quotation (King James Version) from Paul's *Letter to the Galatians* (6:17): the Greek word for 'mark' is *stigma*. But at this point it is difficult to follow Fr Amedeo's account, or Gemma's own words in her *Autobiographia*, without feeling challenged.

Even in Catholic communities, stigmatics have suffered from stigma in its other, more vernacular sense – social rejection. Surely they were faking these wounds? Surely they were also indulging in a form of spiritual pride, taking 'the imitation of Christ' to a blameworthy degree? Surely they were unduly *literalising* the command to take up one's cross?

The corollaries for a biography are evident. If someone fakes stigmata, surely there is little else, in their own account of themselves, that we can trust? If they have duped *some* people (some stigmatics have, of course, been found to have self-inflicted the wounds), can we believe any 'believing' or apologetic biography?

Someone afflicted with the stigmata has mimicked, in his or her own body, the story of the life (more specifically the last hours of the life) of Christ in a way that is shocking. Their body has been taken over – almost parasitised – by someone else's wounds. Christ's bio-graphy (and thanato-graphy) is written into their life story, into their flesh.

In modern times, photographs are taken, and doctors and scientists summoned. Stigmatics, whose wounds tend to occur over the two days of the week (Thursday and Friday) associated with the Passion, are often able to live for long periods without any food other than the Eucharist, of which they partake unusually frequently. This ability is known as *inedia*. It seems dangerously close to the terrifying illness of anorexia. And this, in turn, is inseparable from the enormous problem, today, of the life stories of young women in particular being dominated by questions of body image.

Scientific investigations are somewhat hampered by the relative scarcity of the phenomenon. Dr Edward Hartung studied the case of St Francis of Assisi in 1935 and diagnosed quartan malaria, which caused purpura and ecchymoses. There have been psychiatric studies, especially focusing on stigmata as hysterical symptoms. (In hysteria, the body finds a way of symbolising, in often drastic forms, psychological conflicts.) Anorexics may wound themselves as part of obsessional compulsive behaviour; more widely, the epidemic of self-harming (a prolongation of punk's early fascination with blades and piercings) may be a form of self-stigmatisation. The stigmatic's wounds may be the result of heightened autosuggestibility. And the visions that accompany the bleeding may be part of a dissociative identity disorder. But there is little consensus; and in any case, it is not clear what is proved by the application of such language to the wounds in question (especially since the wounded, notoriously, do not want to be healed, so that recourse to the language of physicians seems oddly irrelevant). Nor are these different 'diagnoses' necessarily mutually exclusive (hysteria may be a religious phenomenon, just as religious 'wounds' may be hysterical; both priest and doctor can come away from the stigmatic feeling equally vindicated).

The recent remarkable book *The Voices of Gemma Galgani. The Life and Afterlife of a Modern Saint*, by Rudolph M. Bell and Cristina Mazzoni (Chicago, 2003) is a rather different kind of biography from Fr Amedeo's, since it is subtended by all these questions (by *our* 'Higher Criticism', or Theory). Bell and Mazzoni state: 'Gemma Galgani is a compelling saint in so many ways: confident, grandiose, manipulative, childish, abandoned, loved, complicated, simple-minded, admired, forgotten.' She is a modern saint (the first person who lived into the twentieth century to be beatified and then, on 2 May 1940, when the mind of Europe was largely occupied with grimmer matters, canonised). She is also timeless: a stigmatic who saw Jesus as her 'spiritual lover' and the Virgin Mary as her 'Mom', while her guardian angel delivered her letters from Lucca to her spiritual director and later biographer, Fr Germano, in Rome.[12]

Their biography does not begin with Gemma's photo staring at us, but it does include a much wider range of photos, including one posed and retouched (Gemma with hands clasped in prayer, gazing upwards, with a halo), and what is claimed as 'the most authentic photo of her as an adult' in which she presents a strikingly different persona from the 'prayer card' versions: Gemma is again looking straight at the camera, and in dark clothes, but her head is cocked to one side, her hair is less tightly combed, her cheeks are fuller, almost chubby, and, above all, her smile is much warmer, with almost a hint of full-lipped roguishness. She could be a young woman in a Rohmer film, sizing up a suitor, affectionate and quizzical. The biography by Amedeo is barely mentioned (I do not know whether it is not greatly esteemed in the field of Gemma Galgani studies). The book by Bell and Mazzoni does not come with the burden and protection of an *imprimatur*; instead, we get the affidavits of the scholarly world: a note that Rudolph Bell is a professor at Rutgers, and has written *Holy Anorexia* among other books, while Cristina Mazzoni is at Vermont, and her works include *Saint Hysteria: Neurosis, Mysticism and Gender in European Culture*. The authors include a nice dedication to family members, and 'acknowledgments' that remind us how every piece of writing is a collective endeavour. Then an introduction, beginning with an epigraph: words of Jesus to Gemma in March 1901, predicting that she would be a saint. In this introduction, like many good biographers, the authors say how and why they became interested in their biographee, how they might have changed their minds about the best way to approach her, and how they were eventually forced to acknowledge that 'the *trans*cendency of Gemma's life calls for a *trans*disciplinary strategy'.

They therefore share out the chapters between them: Bell writes more as a historian; Mazzoni more as a literary critic. There are chapters that place Gemma in the context of church-state rivalries, especially in Lucca. There are large swathes of Gemma's own writing – her autobiography, her diary, and her letters. These are Gemma's 'voices', and the voices that spoke to her and through her. In Part Two, these writings are examined: how did Gemma become a saint? How was she manipulated by male clerics?

One question that subtends this, as all biographies, must be: to what extent is the biographee a role model? What kind of role model is favoured by what age groups (and genders), in what ages, and why? Is Madonna a role model? Is the Madonna a role model?[13]

And finally, how can a feminist approach such a troubling figure? This last section is called 'A Saint's Alphabet' and focuses on key words (autobiography, body, clothes, Dad, Eucharist, food…) to capture the many ways in which Gemma's experience can be interpreted. Was she a masochist? Was her suffering the result of patriarchal oppression? To what extent are her writings examples of Cixous' *Écriture feminine* or Kristeva's 'pre-semiotic'? Was she a cyborg, of the kind hymned by Donna Haraway? Was she an exemplar of Foucauldian transgression? Of Irigarayan mysticism? The book ends in Mazzoni's powerful address *to* her biographee, a letter to 'my dear Gemma Galgani' that keeps open all the issues raised by modern theoretical discourse – all of these voices are and are not 'Gemma's' – while releasing Gemma from all such biographical strategies; she is no longer a 'she' but a 'you'.

When Gemma Galgani died, the nuns keeping vigil had to struggle to keep the crowds of her devotees from stripping every relic-worthy hair off her head; later, Fr Germano ensured that her buried body was exhumed. It was found to have an unusually large heart that looked as fresh as a living one.[14]

Life of Jean Genet

I first read the name of Saint Marguerite Marie Alacoque, a novena to whom cured Gemma Galgani, in Sartre's *Saint Genet, Actor and Martyr*. Here, Alacoque is cited as a woman who took abjection seriously. She showed solicitude even for the most bracingly excrementitious aspects of human life: she respected, not just the face of the other, but his faeces as well. She thus provided a 'parallel life' for Genet, who revelled morosely in everything that seemed the negative of bourgeois society.

Gemma Galgani aspired to be a Passionist. Sartre describes Genet as a *'passéiste'*: essentially someone who chooses to remain imprisoned by the past. In many of his biographical essays, including the vast *The Family Idiot*, in which he tries to show what can be known of a singular individual (Flaubert) in the light of modern theories (especially existential psychoanalysis tinged with a Marxist analysis of class), Sartre attempts to uncover an original 'trauma' which the biographee chose (actively/passively) as determining his life. In Genet's case, this was a trauma of naming. The boy Genet indulged in petty pilfering; he was labelled a 'thief' (a verb, 'thieving', was converted into a noun); he then chose to identify himself as such, in an act of perverse defiance. He would *be* a thief, and be it in a spectacular way. The same happened when he sensed that he was an outsider in another sense: he would *be* a homosexual, *jusqu'au bout*. For Sartre, Genet's biography is the unfolding of these original choices. *Saint* Genet? This is *partly* a joke; *Saint Genest* was the title of a work of early modern French literature.

Derrida's *Glas* is in many ways a rejoinder to Sartre, focusing on the wordplay that subtends and distorts Genet's shifting sense of identity. *Glas* is also a Plutarchan parallel life: on opposite pages we are given a reading of Hegel and of Genet respectively. Which is the more subversive? (Derrida, naturally, plays fast and loose with the notion of biography: he draws on Hegel's letters, his relations with his sister, his family life, etc., and also incorporates material from Genet's conversations with him. But these data are then processed in curious ways.)

Faced with Sartre's biography, Genet, for a while, fell silent. He thought that Sartre had pinned him down and explained his life so eloquently that there was nothing more to say. He had a similar reaction to Derrida's work. To be eviscerated so thoroughly by two of the greatest French philosophers of modern times was unnerving, however great his friendship and admiration for them both. A biography, however experimental, cannot help but co-opt its subject: Sartre names Genet's shame, Derrida lays bare the signifiers from which his career is suspended – they both perform the act which Genet so frequently extolled, that of betrayal. By betraying him, they are thus being faithful to him. (Yet again, it is Judas who writes the biography – it seems to be an essential moment in what might be called the 'economy' of salvation.)

In 1989, Harry E. Stewart and Rob Roy Macgregor published *Jean Genet: A Biography of Deceit, 1910–1951*. They resorted to Genet's prison records, army files, medical reports, interviews with childhood friends, and many other 'objective' accounts, to show how Genet had mythologised his own life.[15] Biographers had sometimes taken him at face value; or perhaps he had just been living up to biographers' expectations, stealing his existence together from this and that (as Beethoven said of one of his works).

Part II
Rulers, Warlords and Rebels

Life of Shih Huang Di

Sima Qian's *Historical Records* contained many short biographies of rulers and others who were close to those in power. His work is fascinating for the way it gathers so many individuals into categories. There are generals (Sun Tzu), including a sub-category of 'maligned generals'; there are politicians; there are philosophers (Laozi, Mozi). There are collective biographies of disciples of Confucius, different sorts of barbarians, benevolent officials, and assassins. There are 'cruel officials', 'wandering knights', 'the forest of scholars', flatterers, humorists, sooth-sayers, diviners, and profiteers. There are also historians (and an autobiography of the Grand Scribe, Sima Qian himself, as well as a biography of his father, Sima Tan, whose work as a historian he had continued).

The memoirs that comprise these biographies are known as *liezhuan* or 'exemplary lives', and they tend to select those deeds that show exactly how exemplary their subject was, though they also add legendary accounts of less evidently moralistic character.

The first emperor of a united China, the one who burnt the books and built the wall, was Qin Shih Huang. His symbols were – we are told – water, the number six, and the colour black. He was advised by his ministers to call himself *Zhen*, the mysterious one. His reign was troubled. The chief minister submitted a memo to him: scholars, he pointed out, were using records from the past to criticise the present. (This is always the danger with history in general and with biographies in particular.)

> Your servant requests that all who possess literature such as the *Songs*, the *Documents*, and the sayings of the hundred schools should get rid of it without penalty. If they have not got rid of it a full thirty days after the order has reached them, they should be branded and sent to do forced labour on the walls [the Great Wall]. There should be exemption for books concerned with medicine, pharmacy, divination by tortoiseshell and milfoil, the sowing of crops, and the planting of trees. If there are those who wish to study, they should take the law officers as their teachers.
>
> Approving his proposals, the First Emperor collected up and got rid of the *Songs*, the *Documents*, and the sayings of the hundred schools in order to make the people stupid and ensure that in all under Heaven there should be no rejection of the present by using the past. The clarification of laws and regulations and the settling of statutes and ordinances all started with the Emperor. He documents. Lodges to be occupied during his travels were erected, and he made extensive journeys throughout the Empire. In the following year he again made a tour of inspection and drove out the barbarians on all four sides (tr. Raymond Dawson).

The books were thus burnt – but copies of them were kept in the Imperial Library (though, at the end of the Qin dynasty, which followed soon after Qin Shih Huang's own death in 210 BC and the subsequent turmoil, this library itself went up in flames. Fortunately, some copies had been hidden by scholars, and some of the works had been memorised). Qin Shih Huang, in any case, was not so concerned with how he lived on in the records of his annalists. Or rather, this *did* concern him – but he also sought a more concrete form of immortality. Dreading death, he spent much of his reign in a quest for the Daoist elixir of immortality. He did not want to live on in his work. He wanted to live on by not dying. It was while he was in the middle of such a quest, far from his capital, that he did in fact die.

Sima Qian, in his *Shiji*, tells us a great deal about what this emperor did – and about what emperors in general could expect to do. There is a repertoire of 'things done by an emperor', and each imperial life will contain these in various combinations. We can compare accounts in the *Shiji* with the somewhat dryer and more formulaic versions in the *Hanshu*, the official history of the Han dynasty, to form a composite picture of what one emperor did. He travelled east and inspected the sea-coast. He made sacrifices to the Eight Spirits. He pondered the words of the scholars and magicians concerning the right offerings to be made; then he made the requisite sacrifices, dressed in yellow robes. On the day prescribed, he ordered the official secretaries to don their leather caps and perform the ritual shooting of oxen. He fixed official titles; he harmonised the sounds of the musical pipes. He sent out his generals to build fortresses. On his return from sacrifices, he sat in the Clear Hall, and all the officials wished him long life.

These, at least, are some of the deeds of the Filial Emperor Xiao Wudi (the Martial), Son of Heaven, who reigned 140–87 BC. They are, to anyone who does not know enough of ancient Chinese history to put flesh on the bones, pure denotation – the uninitiated reader does not know how to evaluate this information. Is Xiao Wudi being particularly pious, or just as pious as expected? Did all emperors pay such attention to music? Did the eastern sea-coast need inspecting, and of what did the inspection consist? A Sinologist may know the answer to these questions, but to a 'profane' reader, the notations of these old biographies have all the poetry of the exotic. Sima Qian, who had been punished by the imperial courts for some misdemeanour, was offered the choice of death or castration. He chose the latter, which condemned him to a life of shame. It has been argued (for instance by John Man) that Sima Qian's biographies were secretly tendentious: he did indeed write 'exemplary' lives of previous emperors to criticise the current emperor. It has also been noted that he tended to omit references to the supernatural powers of the heroes whose lives he narrated. Perhaps he was a debunker – the Lytton Strachey of ancient China? On the other hand, he may have turned what were originally gods and spirits into apparently historical figures, thereby confusing categories: secularising the supernatural (an enlightened thing to do) but creating historical characters who did not, in fact, exist. (This heroisation of the sacred happens frequently; when a culture pays ritual homage to its founders, or its role models, the boundary between sacred and non-sacred becomes porous, as does that between myth and history. And however much desacralisation seems to bring down the stars to earth, the dialectical result is often that the earth becomes even more starry-eyed than before.)

Because of Qin Shih Huang's burning of the books, there may well be gaps in our knowledge of the biographies of his predecessors. How can we fill in these gaps? Should we? Ezra Pound praised Chinese historians for leaving a blank when they were not sure of their facts. Sima Qian was one of these. 'I have written down only what is certain, and in doubtful cases, I have left a blank.' Nonetheless, the relative reliability of much of his record is attested by no less a Sinologist than Joseph Needham. Even though he was writing about events that had occurred 1,000 years before his own day, twenty-three of the thirty Shang kings listed by Sima Qian are found recorded on oracle bones that have been excavated at the Shang dynasty capital, at Anyang (Yinxu). Even the most ancient of biographies do not stand alone: lives and their traces are hidden in the earth, and can arise at any moment.

Life of Catiline

Sallust, at the beginning of his account of the Jugurthine War, dwells on the right and wrong ways to court fame. For this is what they were after, those ancients: Greek *kleos*, with its etymology of that which gleams, or Latin *fama*, linked to the word fate and that which is spoken. You live on, not just as a shade in the concourse of Hades, but in the gleaming words of blind poets and sober chroniclers. History-writing was of crucial importance for one's written survival; it was like a wax mask, acting as a stimulus to the ambitious:

Men unreasonably complain about their nature – that, being weak and short-lived, it is governed by chance rather than intellectual power. On the contrary, you will find, upon reflection, that there is nothing more noble or excellent [...] The ruler and director of the life of man is the mind [*animus*], which, when it pursues glory along the path of true merit, is sufficiently powerful, efficient, and worthy of honour, and needs no assistance from fortune, which can neither bestow integrity, industry, or other good qualities, nor take them away. But if the mind, ensnared by corrupt passions, abandons itself to indolence and sensuality, when it has indulged in pernicious gratifications for a while, and when bodily strength, time, and mental vigour have been wasted in sloth, it is the infirmity of nature that is accused – and those who are themselves at fault blame their shortcomings on circumstances.

This is a short exposition of the dialectic between freedom and determinism. How does a man become the person that he is? What is the balance between nature and nurture? How far can the 'mind' (*animus* – the Latin word also means spirit, as in high-spirited) govern a life, and how far is life ruled by contingency? What is the part played by social factors and other 'circumstances'?

Sallust goes on to make a pitch for his own profession: that of historian. 'Among other intellectual employments, the recording of past events is of pre-eminent utility.' He has already tried his hand at public office, but has now retired from the fray. There is considerable evidence, even in his own account, that Sallust had fallen prey to the corruption of public life in Rome that his writings denounce. His works, indeed, are the account of a man now going straight: he will be all the better a judge of a wicked world that he knows from the inside. He has retired from that world to see it from above; he has exchanged the active for the (equally useful) contemplative life. As he puts it, in more neutral tones, the world needs its secretaries, and heroes need their biographers – who are thus worth just as much to the republic as those who lead a more active life. Quintus Maximus and Publius Scipio had observed how, 'when they looked at images of their ancestors, they felt their minds irresistibly stimulated to the pursuit of honour'. Not of course that a wax bust itself had any such influence; it served merely as a reminder of what a man could achieve. The biographer can produce a similar wax bust. He can also present his contemporaries with examples to avoid, as in Sallust's biography of Catiline, in which the writer makes the same proud (not to say arrogant) boast that, essentially, the biographer alone can confer fame – or notoriety. In his diatribe against Catiline, we may surmise, the biographer knew what he was talking about.

All men, he begins, should strive to excel, not like the animals which grovel in obscurity, feeding their appetites alone. Mind is what brings us closer to the gods, and 'since the life which we enjoy is short', we should 'make the remembrance of us as lasting as possible. For the glory of wealth and beauty is fleeting and perishable; that of intellectual power is illustrious and immortal.' A biographer is a writer, that is, someone whose life is an uneasy mix of the active and the contemplative. Indeed, continues Sallust, 'he only seems to me to live, and to enjoy life, who, intent upon some employment, seeks reputation from some ennobling enterprise, or honourable pursuit'. But he now looks back on his own life: in an autobiographical hint that would have been clearer to his contemporaries, he now condemns his earlier political activities as the result of a 'corrupt ambition' luring him from the studies to which he is now returning. Uninfluenced, he says, by fear, hope, or political partisanship, he will 'give a brief account, with as much truth as I can, of the Conspiracy of Catiline; for I think it an enterprise eminently deserving of record, from the unusual nature both of guilt and of the perils involved in it. But before I enter upon my narrative, I must give a short description of the character of the man.'

Catiline, says Sallust, was of noble birth, and had many fine qualities, but he had 'a vicious and depraved disposition'. From his youth onwards, Catiline took delight in 'civil commotions, bloodshed, robbery, and sedition'. His 'constitution could endure hunger, lack of sleep, and cold, to a degree surpassing belief. His mind was daring, subtle, and versatile, capable of pretending or dissembling whatever he wished. He was covetous of other men's property, and prodigal of his own. He had abundance of eloquence, though but little wisdom. His insatiable ambition was always pursuing objects that were extravagant, romantic, and unattainable.'

Here, as in many 'lives' of the Greek and Roman world, the biographee is judged first: we are presented right at the start with a character-sketch, and the narrative then gives examples to support this initial opinion. The character of Catiline is immediately complex: he is not a double-dyed villain, but a man whose moral ambiguities are made to fall into antithetical patterns, in a rhetoric of balanced assessment (his body is tough but his mind is subtle; he was covetous but prodigal; he was eloquent but lacked wisdom). These patterns are set out in sentences that remind us how much the mind of Roman men was keyed to the syntax of Latin, and engineered to perform efficiently in the public arena, especially a court of law. Sallust's words here almost sound like the summing-up of a modern QC, even though the abstractions ('constitution', 'mind', 'covetous', 'prodigal', 'eloquent', 'wisdom') have yet to be saturated by anything concrete.

Catiline, we are told, wanted power, and did not much care how he got it. He had several motives. As his patrimony waned, his 'violent spirit' was urged on; he was also conscious of the guilt he had already accrued (what we might call the 'Macbeth Argument': 'I am in blood stepp'd in so far…'). Sallust mentions another motive: 'the corrupt morals of the state'. These two were conflicting vices ('extravagance and [i.e. pulling against] selfishness') and yet their joint influence impelled Catiline further into the mire of intrigue.

At this point, Sallust steps back for a moment from his hero-villain to describe how Rome had declined from its rustic virtues into luxury and decadence – a *topos* almost as old as Rome itself. Catiline is a particularly vicious example of a general depravity. He thus found it easy to attract men of similar baseness to him.

> In so populous and so corrupt a city, Catiline, as it was very easy to do, kept about him, like a body-guard, crowds of the unprincipled and desperate. For all those shameless, libertine, and profligate characters, who had dissipated their patrimonies by gambling, luxury, and sensuality; all who had contracted heavy debts, to purchase immunity for their crimes or offenses; all assassins or sacrilegious persons from every quarter, convicted or dreading conviction for their evil deeds; all, besides, whom their tongue or their hand maintained by perjury or civil bloodshed; all, in fine, whom wickedness, poverty, or a guilty conscience disquieted, were the associates and intimate friends of Catiline. And if any one, as yet of unblemished character, fell into his society, he was presently rendered, by daily intercourse and temptation, similar and equal to the rest.

Catiline, as it were, merely becomes a metonym for a host of debauched men. He seduced the young in particular, procuring mistresses for some, horses and dogs for others, money for the rest; the young, after all, are hot-blooded enough to want these things, and easily led (though Sallust says there is no evidence that some of them practised 'crimes against nature', so his group portrayal is not a piece of propaganda that seizes on every potential calumny).

Sallust continues: 'Catiline, in his youth, had been guilty of many criminal connections, with a virgin of noble birth, with a priestess of Vesta, and of many other offenses of this nature, in defiance alike of law and religion.' The first two offences, against class and religion (which were closely related), were particularly heinous; we are left to guess at the 'many others'. Then Catiline fell for a woman, Aurelia Orestilla, whose only recommendation, in the eyes of 'any good man' (in which category Sallust tacitly includes himself and enrols his reader), was her beauty. When she hesitated, 'it is confidently believed' that, because she did not want a grown-up stepson, Catiline put his son to death.

This produces a passage of celebrated vividness; a portrait of a criminal who feels that, ethically speaking, he has nothing left to lose.

> For his guilty mind, at peace with neither gods nor men, found no comfort either waking or sleeping; so effectually did conscience desolate his tortured spirit. His complexion, in consequence, was pale, his eyes haggard, his walk sometimes quick and sometimes slow, and distraction was plainly apparent in every feature and look.

Sallust captures the turmoil of his biographee in one telling, concrete detail: 'his walk sometimes quick and sometimes slow'. The rest of the *Conspiracy of Catiline* is in a sense a long coda to this description, in which the full implications of Catiline's mixture of hesitancy and precipitation, of impetuousness and occasional panic, are fully developed. Moral behaviour is a matter of tempo. A biographer needs to focus on the moments when the action speeds up and slows down, and the way the biographee's own velocity is counterpointed with this. Sallust has also been selective, tendentious, moralising, and more than a little hypocritical. Nobody ever quite retires from a life of corruption.

The translator of Sallust, the vicar John Selby Watson, was also a biographer (of George Fox, John Wilkes, and William Cobbett), and a productive but impecunious scholar. When, for obscure reasons, he beat his wife to death with his pistol butt, before attempting to poison himself with prussic acid, he was at first found guilty of murder, and sentenced to death. This was subsequently commuted, on the (then quite novel) grounds of 'temporary insanity'. Perhaps there are moments in a life which are simply illegible? Things suddenly speed up and fall apart: biography, that leisurely, appraising genre, can never really do justice to these tragic accelerandi. Beryl Bainbridge produced a *biographie romancée* of this troubled figure in her *Watson's Apology* (1984).

Life of Augustus

IMPERATORI CAESARI DIVI FILIO AUGUSTO begins the inscription on the great monument at La Turbie, in the hills behind Monaco, overlooking the Mediterranean: 'To the Emperor Augustus, son [actually adoptive] of the deified Caesar [i.e. Julius]'. There follows a list of his titles, and then an explanation for the presence of the monument: *QUOD EIUS DUCTU AUSPICIISQUE GENTES ALPINAE OMNES QUA A MARI SUPERO AD INFERUM PERTINEBANT SUB IMPERIUM POPULI ROMANI SUNT REDACTAE*: 'because, under his leadership and auspices, all the Alpine tribes found between the Upper Sea and the Lower have been brought under the dominion of the Roman People'. There follows a catalogue of all the defeated tribes.

Monuments (and inscriptions: lithographies, or stone-writings, of every kind) are often a major source for the biographies of ancient rulers. This one marks a high point (in all senses) of Augustus' career. The vanquishing of the tribes who lived between Gaul and Italy meant that, in this direction, Roman territory was now unified right across the Alps; and Augustus was the ruler who had, after decades of civil war, brought what was now an empire under his control.

The way the image of the emperors of Rome was managed, by coinage, inscription, and statuary, has become a staple among historians of the ancient world. It has provided a template ever since: the paraphernalia of Roman imperial might have been co-opted by every kind of regime. On his death (AD 14), it was a funerary inscription which catalogued his deeds; it is known as the *Res Gestae Divi Augusti* (the 'things achieved by the deified Augustus' – from Julius Caesar onwards, Roman rulers were, throughout the pagan era, generally deified after their deaths). It had been composed during Augustus' lifetime (he left a copy with his will) and naturally gives a positive view of his reign: copies of it were set up throughout the empire. It also elides the fact that Augustus' principate was, in spite of his lip-service to the old republic and his claims to have restored rather than revolutionised Rome, the absolute rule of a single man, backed by religious sanction.

In the *Res Gestae*, Augustus' deeds are narrated in the first person (making the inscription similar to those of the pharaohs). The document falls into four main sections: his political career; his benefactions (money, land, grain, gladiatorial shows); his military deeds; and the plaudits of his people. There is a third-person appendix adding details on his building projects. (This last section may well not have been overseen by Augustus himself.) The original (now lost) was inscribed on two bronze pillars (now lost) which stood before his mausoleum.

This piece of (auto)biography as imperial propaganda is something of a template for the 'good ruler'. 'The people', that most crucial yet nebulous of Roman concepts, is constantly evoked as being the object of Augustus' solicitude and a reservoir of support for his deeds. He did the Virgilian thing (*'parcere subiectis et debellare superbos'*):[16] 'I often waged war, civil and foreign, on the earth and sea, in the whole wide world, and as victor I spared all the citizens who sought pardon. As for foreign nations, those which I was able to safely forgive, I preferred to preserve than to destroy.' (Horace said, 'All the earth is Roman earth': it seemed that way.) He made sure the religious proprieties were observed: 'On account of the things success-fully done by me and through my officers, under my auspices, on earth and sea, the senate decreed fifty-five times that there be sacrifices to the immortal gods.' He was loth to rush into office; he needed to be persuaded into power; but he did not evade his responsibilities:

> When the dictatorship was offered to me, both in my presence and my absence, by the people and senate, when Marcus Marcellus and Lucius Arruntius were consuls [22 BC] I did not accept it. I did not evade the curatorship of grain in the height of the food shortage, which I so arranged that within a few days I freed the entire city from the present fear and danger by my own expense and administration. When the annual and perpetual consulate was then again offered to me, I did not accept it.

He was generous with his money:

> I paid to the Roman plebs, HS 300 [300 sesterces] per man from my father's will and in my own name gave HS 400 from the spoils of war when I was consul for the fifth time [29 BC]; furthermore I again paid out a public gift of HS 400 per man, in my tenth consulate [24 BC], from my own patrimony; and, when consul for the eleventh time [23 BC], twelve doles of grain personally bought were measured

out; and in my twelfth year of tribunician power [12–11 BC] I gave HS 400 per man for the third time. And these public gifts of mine never reached fewer than 250,000 men. In my eighteenth year of tribunician power, as consul for the twelfth time [5 BC], I gave to 320,000 plebs of the city HS 240 per man. And, when consul the fifth time [29 BC], I gave from my war-spoils to colonies of my soldiers each HS 1,000 per man; about 120,000 men in the colonies received this triumphal public gift. Consul for the thirteenth time [2 BC], I gave HS 240 to the plebs who then received the public grain; they were a few more than 200,000.

And he entertained:

Three times I gave shows of gladiators under my name and five times under the name of my sons and grandsons; in these shows about 10,000 men fought. Twice I furnished under my name spectacles of athletes gathered from everywhere, and three times under my grandson's name. [...] Twenty-six times, under my name or that of my sons and grandsons, I gave the people hunts of African beasts in the circus, in the open, or in the amphitheatre; in them about 3,500 beasts were killed. I gave the people a spectacle of a naval battle, in the place across the Tiber where the grove of the Caesars is now, with the ground excavated in length 1,800 feet, in width 1,200, in which thirty beaked ships, biremes or triremes, but many smaller, fought among themselves; in these ships about 3,000 men fought in addition to the rowers.

(The detailed nature of this account is curious: a good emperor would hereafter want to be remembered for the number of beasts he had killed in the circuses.) He built, as the third-person appendix puts it, the temples of Mars, of Jupiter Subduer and Thunderer, of Apollo, of divine Julius, of Minerva, of Queen Juno, of Jupiter Liberator, of the Lares, of the gods of the Penates, of Youth, and of the Great Mother, the Lupercal, the state box at the circus, the senate-house with the Chalcidicum, the forum of Augustus, the Julian basilica, the theatre of Marcellus, the Octavian portico, and the grove of the Caesars across the Tiber. He rebuilt the Capitol and holy temples numbering eighty-two, the theatre of Pompey, waterways, and the Flaminian road.

And, as we have seen, he pacified hitherto unruly lands: 'I brought peace to the Alps from the region which is near the Adriatic Sea to the Tuscan', adding – not that he had any need to be defensive – 'with no unjust war waged against any nation'.

Such was the CV with which Augustus applied for earthly immortality. (*Lives of the Caesars* by Suetonius suggests one reason for interest in the lives of rulers: what do people do when they have power, especially when they have absolute power?)

Lives of Later Roman Emperors

The later emperors would have their panegyrists. More long-winded than the dry but imperious account in the *Res Gestae*, they extolled at length the virtues of the emperors to whom they were addressed. Panegyrics were a common rhetorical exercise: when St Augustine was official rhetor in Milan, it was part of his job to deliver a panegyric to the emperor. (This would have been Valentinian II, who held court in Milan from 375–87.) Augustine obliged. But, in the *Confessions*, he looked back on the episode with some cynicism. By the time he wrote this work he wanted to address panegyrics to nobody except the work's addressee, God:

How wretched I was then, and you dealt with me in such a way as to make me aware of my wretchedness on the day I was preparing to deliver a panegyric on the Emperor, in which I would put forward many lies, and my lies would be applauded by those who knew I was lying; and my heart panted with these anxieties, and boiled over with the fever of all-consuming thoughts. (*Confessions*, book 6, ch. 6)

When Valentinian died in Vienne, the circumstances were a little mysterious: he was found hanged in his rooms. Ambrose was on his way to Vienne to baptise him, but was too late. The emperor may have been murdered by Arbogast the Frank; it is more probable that he committed suicide. Ambrose wrote a eulogy of him (or 'consolation': *De obitu Valentiniani consolatio*),which tactfully left the matter open, since he wanted to present the dead emperor as a model of Christian virtue.

Latinus Pacatus Drepanius lived at the end of the fourth century; he was a professor of rhetoric at Burdigala (Bordeaux), and achieved high office (in 390 he was proconsul of Africa). In 389, in the Senate in Rome, he gave a famous panegyric on Emperor Theodosius I. It opens by saying how filled the orator is with 'fear and trembling', and apologises for the speaker's 'Transalpine mode of speech' (he was from the south of France) – conventional modes of *captatio benevolentiae*. He moves on to a chronological account of Theodosius' career from his accession (19 January 379) onwards. We have seen the *Res Gestae* not exactly as an autobiography but as a biography in the first person; a panegyric of this kind is a biography in the second person. The modern reader finds this account difficult to follow: verbose, stuffed with rhetorical questions, and weighed down with high-flown parallels from the past: 'Africanus did not endure so patiently his first military apprenticeship under his father Paulus, nor did Hannibal as a boy follow the tents in Spain with an equal talent, nor did Alexander – not yet the Great – fill the camps of Philip with a surer hope of future valour'; in other words, you, emperor, showed military promise while still a boy. He had merited his appointment as emperor, yet he had not sought it. (Just like Augustus: such a topos, or commonplace, that it had its own name: *recusatio imperii* or 'turning down supreme power', when everyone knows you want it: Julius Caesar waving away the crown, though with increasing reluctance...). Nothing the emperor does is without its parallel from the past. 'What Hortensius or Lucullus or Caesar ever had such a ready memory as your sacred mind?' The specifics of Theodosius' reign are swallowed up in vast generalisations: 'Divine beings surely enjoy perpetual motion, and eternity maintains its energy by continuous activity, and whatever we mortals call work is your nature'; and his dominion extends into vague immensities, as his might reaches parts of the world that other emperors have not reached, since even apparently inaccessible regions now tremble: 'The Ocean does not make the Indian secure, nor the cold the man from Bosphorus, nor the equatorial sun the Arab.' But as the panegyric progresses it gradually becomes more concrete and more vivid; and this is largely the result of Pacatus introducing the villain of his piece, Maximus. This man, known also as Magnus Maximus ('Great Greatest' – more fully Flavius Magnus Maximus), was a usurper who launched a campaign from Britain. Pacatus' emollient tones can now turn to catcalls; his panegyric can come to life because it can also include a 'negative biography', or diatribe. Here is Maximus, plundering Pacatus' own land of Gaul:

To Maximus, however, all methods of earning praise seemed foolish. In defiance of the model of virtue which is implanted even in the worst of men, he defined his supreme happiness in terms of acquiring things and doing harm, and not only sought to have as much as possible, but laboured to ensure that nothing was left for anyone else. For he did not, as is customary with kings, watch over the workings of the mines in order to fetch out for his use the hidden bounties of Nature and acquire a fortune which harmed nobody and left none the poorer [...] he thought purer and more splendid that gold which grieving men had given, which had been bathed not by river waters but by the tears of men, which had not been extracted from underground tunnels, but torn from the necks and throats of the slain.

Every biography will have its villains, or at least those who hindered the biographee on his or her rise to becoming – a biographee.

Life of Castruccio Castracani

One of Machiavelli's later works was a biography of the early fourteenth-century warlord Castruccio Castracani. This short piece of writing, typical of Machiavelli in its concision (he is laconic; a true Spartan), was in some ways an experimental 'life'. His account was subsumed into Machiavelli's later *Florentine Histories*, but in his *Life*, Machiavelli explored the new moral universe that he had explored more systematically in *The Prince* and the *Discourses* by focusing on one man who was to some people a villain (a violent and predatory factional leader), and to others (or at least to Machiavelli) a hero, the kind of man Italy, that disunited congeries of petty principalities, city states, and papal domains, needed.

The *Florentine Histories* refer to Castruccio thus:

It was in this period [1316–17: Dante was still alive, but he would never see Florence again] that the lordship of Lucca and Pisa was taken away from Uguccione, and Castruccio Castracani, a citizen of Lucca, became their ruler, and, because he was young, ardent, and fierce, and fortunate in all he undertook, he became in a very short time the leader of the Ghibellines of Tuscany.

The deeds, again, spell out the pre-existing moral dispositions: *because* Castruccio was this type of person, he became leader of the Ghibellines. There is a double causality at work, however: he was also 'fortunate'. It is not explained, in this elliptical account, how his talents were related to his good fortune, but we can assume that Castruccio was one of those men who could take advantage of (or treat with caution) the favours of fortune, which is a keyword in the précis of Castruccio's career that follows. Faced with a big army at Prato, he retreats to Lucca 'without attempting to try his fortune in battle'. The nobles in his party did not want to 'tempt Fortune'. When he finally died, 'since it frequently happens that Fortune accompanies one good or evil with another good or another evil', another man – Charles, Lord of Florence – died in Naples at the same time, so that the Florentines were simultaneously freed from the two men they feared.

Machiavelli spices his *Life of Castruccio* with these same unpredictable seductions of fortune; but he adds another term, *virtù* – virtue, or the Latin *virtus* (essentially the moral qualities of a *vir* or man). The word *virtù* itself is the site of a permanent crisis in moral evaluation: Castruccio, a typical Renaissance warrior, is hardly virtuous in any Christian sense – but that is precisely Machiavelli's point. Perhaps there is a rival sense in which Castruccio is indeed 'virtuous'; perhaps this rival sense is just as viable as the Christian one. So, in *The Prince*, he can indulge in counter-intuitive couplings that strain our understanding of the words he is using, as when he describes Cesare Borgia as displaying *'tanta ferocia e tanta virtù'* in a context which suggests quite clearly that these terms are meant as a compliment. *'Ferocia'* could mean 'independence', but it also meant 'ferocity'; and we know from other sources what kind of man Cesare Borgia was. It is this moral vertigo that gives so much of the *Life of Castruccio* its fascination: it is a biography which, in the 'Machiavellian' way it deploys a single word – *virtù*, forces us to re-evaluate our moral response to the biographee, and indeed to the whole world of Renaissance individualism which he seems to incarnate.

Life of Justinian

In his *Secret History*, Procopius tells of the rationale behind this new and unusual book.

> In what I have written on the Roman wars up to the present point, the story was arranged in chronological order and as completely as the times then permitted. What I shall write now follows a different plan, supplementing the previous formal chronicle with a disclosure of what really happened throughout the Roman Empire. You see, it was not possible, during the life of certain persons, to write the truth of what they did, as a historian should. If I had, their hordes of spies would have found out about it, and they would have put me to a most horrible death. I could not even trust my nearest relatives. That is why I was compelled to hide the real explanation of many matters glossed over in my previous books.

Some biographies are best written post mortem. But he goes on to set out the difficulties that still lie in his path. Will future generations give credence to such a horrifying narrative as his dual biography of the emperor of Byzantium, Justinian, and his wife Theodora? 'As time flows on and my story becomes ancient history, I fear they may think me a writer of fiction, and even put me among the poets.' More seriously, if they believe what he says, will later monarchs not be tempted to mimic the depravity of this wicked couple? But this danger is tempered by the fact that, in his work – as in history – wickedness was punished. And:

who now would know of the unchastened life of Semiramis or the madness of Sardanapalus or Nero, if the record had not thus been written by men of their own times? Besides, even those who suffer similarly from later tyrants will not find this narrative quite unprofitable. For the miserable find comfort in the philosophy that not on them alone has evil fallen.

The chapter headings given to one translation of *The Secret History* are an alluring guide to its contents. Some of them sound like little self-contained moral tales, or fables by a particularly satirical Aesop, laying bare a Byzantium run by fools and knaves. These chapter headings are not given by Procopius, but they are a faithful guide to his querulous and indignant text:

1. How the Great General Belisarius Was Hoodwinked by His Wife
2. How Belated Jealousy Affected Belisarius's Military Judgment
3. Showing the Danger of Interfering with a Woman's Intrigues
4. How Theodora Humiliated the Conqueror of Africa and Italy
5. How Theodora Tricked the General's Daughter
6. Ignorance of the Emperor Justin, and How His Nephew Justinian Was the Virtual Ruler
7. Outrages of the Blues
8. Character and Appearance of Justinian
9. How Theodora, Most Depraved of All Courtesans, Won His Love
10. How Justinian Created a New Law Permitting Him to Marry a Courtesan
11. How the Defender of the Faith Ruined His Subjects
12. Proving That Justinian and Theodora Were Actually Fiends in Human Form

This appetising menu is not belied by the text, the tale of three equally repellent people: Belisarius, Justinian, and Theodora.

At what point does a biographer describe the biographee? And how does he do so? Only after giving us some account of the cruelties of Justinian does Procopius give us a pen-portrait that rapidly veers from physical to moral description:

> I think this is as good a time as any to describe the personal appearance of the man. Now in physique he was neither

tall nor short, but of average height; not thin, but moderately plump; his face was round, and not bad looking, for he had a good complexion, even when he fasted for two days. To make a long description short, he much resembled Domitian, Vespasian's son. He was the one whom the Romans so hated that even tearing him into pieces did not satisfy their wrath against him, but a decree was passed by the Senate that the name of this Emperor should never be written, and that no statue of him should be preserved. And so this name was erased in all the inscriptions at Rome and wherever else it had been written, except only where it occurs in the list of emperors; and nowhere may be seen any statue of him in all the Roman Empire, save one in brass...

The reason for the survival of this one statue is curious. When Domitian had been butchered, his widow – herself a blameless woman – was allowed by the Senate to ask them one favour.

Now the lady, wishing to leave a memorial to future time of the savagery of those who had butchered her husband, conceived this plan: collecting the pieces of Domitian's body, she joined them accurately together and sewed the body up again into its original semblance. Taking this to the statue makers, she ordered them to produce the miserable form in brass. So the artisans forthwith made the image, and the wife took it, and set it up in the street which leads to the Capitol, on the right hand side as one goes there from the Forum: a monument to Domitian and a revelation of the manner of his death until this day.

Justinian's entire person, his manner of expression and all of his features might be clearly pointed out in this statue.

A biography is a statue made up of *disjecta membra*. The brass statue of Domitian was both a memorial of him and a standing rebuke to the Romans who had murdered him. Because it survived, and was described several times over, Procopius was able to use it as a vivid piece of shorthand. He starts off describing Justinian in a fairly unremarkable way, and even suggests he was not bad-looking. (Those who have seen the mosaic of Justinian in San Vitale, Ravenna, will have their own mental picture of the emperor: handsome, no doubt, in a swarthy, ill-shaven, slightly thuggish way, staring you full in the face; and, unlike the Byzantine courtiers of his own day, you can return his insolent stare.) But he soon bores of this and goes for a comparison that is indistinguishably physical and moral, with a despised emperor who came to a terrible end. (*Damnatio memoriae* – of the kind imposed on Domitian – means, so to speak, that not even a 'negative' biography of you survives; you are erased, as the heretical emperor Akhenaten was by his successor pharaoh from all the monuments of Egypt, and as Falieri was from the Doges' Palace in Venice – dropped into a memory hole. Fortunately or not, history has ways of recovering such erased data and we now know rather a lot about Domitian – and, thanks to Procopius, about his spiritual successor and fellow-reprobate, Justinian.)

Now such was Justinian in appearance; but his character was something I could not fully describe. For he was at once villainous and amenable; as people say colloquially, a moron. He was never truthful with anyone, but always guileful in what he said and did, yet easily hoodwinked by any who wanted to deceive him. His nature was an unnatural mixture of folly and wickedness. What in olden times a peripatetic philosopher said was also true of him, that opposite qualities combine in a man as in the mixing of colours. I will try to portray him, however, insofar as I can fathom his complexity.

This Emperor, then, was deceitful, devious, false, hypocritical, two-faced, cruel, skilled in dissembling his thought, never moved to tears by either joy or pain, though he could summon them artfully at will when the occasion demanded, a liar always, not only offhand, but in writing, and when he swore sacred oaths to his subjects in their very hearing. Then he would immediately break his agreements and pledges, like the vilest of slaves, whom indeed only the fear of torture drives to confess their perjury. A faithless friend, he was a treacherous enemy, insane for murder and plunder, quarrelsome and revolutionary, easily led to anything evil, but never willing to listen to good counsel, quick to plan mischief and carry it out, but finding even the hearing of anything good distasteful to his ears. [...] If one wished to take all the calamities which had befallen the Romans before this time and weigh them against his crimes, I think it would be found that more men had been murdered by this single man than in all previous history.

So much for the *autokrator* of Byzantium, that empire of images, the second Rome, the cradle of orthodoxy, the holy city of the Eastern Christians. It is no wonder that Procopius' account appealed so strongly to Gibbon. (Theodora, his empress, is an equally colourful character, but the way that, from humble beginnings – she was roughly equivalent to a lapdancer-cum-call girl – she worked her way up to imperial consort cannot fail to compel admiration.)

Life of Frederick the Great

It is one of the greatest *incipits* of any biography.

Chapter I: PROEM: FRIEDRICH'S HISTORY FROM THE DISTANCE WE ARE AT.

About fourscore years ago, there used to be seen sauntering on the terraces of Sans Souci, for a short time in the afternoon, or you might have met him elsewhere at an earlier hour, riding or driving in a rapid business manner on the open roads or through the scraggy woods and avenues of that intricate amphibious Potsdam region, a highly interesting lean little old man, of alert though slightly stooping figure; whose name among strangers was King FRIEDRICH THE SECOND, or Frederick the Great of Prussia, and at home among the common people, who much loved and esteemed him, was VATER FRITZ, – Father Fred, – a name of familiarity which had not bred contempt in that instance. He is a King every inch of him, though without the trappings of a King. Presents himself in a Spartan simplicity of vesture: no crown but an old military cocked-hat, – generally old, or trampled and kneaded into absolute SOFTNESS, if new; – no sceptre but one like Agamemnon's, a walking-stick cut from the woods, which serves also as a riding-stick (with which he hits the horse 'between the ears,' say authors); – and for royal robes, a mere soldier's blue coat with red facings, coat likely to be old, and sure to have a good deal of Spanish snuff on the breast of it; rest of the apparel dim, unobtrusive in colour or out, ending in high over-knee military boots, which may be brushed (and, I hope, kept soft with an underhand suspicion of oil), but are not permitted to be blackened or varnished; Day and Martin with their soot-pots forbidden to approach.

The king leaps from the page in these two sentences (and what sentences!); every aspect of Carlyle's style is aimed at bridging the fourscore years between the reader and Frederick. It seems as casual ('sans souci') as the king himself, allowing for different possibilities ('or you [a nice apostrophe to the reader, who is transported to that distant place] might have met him elsewhere', 'riding or driving', 'on the open roads or through the scraggy woods'). The man has many names, and though they all have the same reference, their sense is in every case different; he is defined relationally, and none of his attributes exhaust him, since – as Carlyle immediately goes on to suggest – each of them can be unpacked in often disconcerting ways. So he is a 'King every inch of him, though without the trappings of a King'. A cloud passes briefly over the text – is this a *fallen* king, like Lear? No, and nor is he mad – but he is eccentric enough to deviate from the model of kingship laid down in the tradition, and the rest of Carlyle's biography shows how this unkingly king, who belonged so little to the 'unhistorical' eighteenth century in which he lived, was at the same time one of its most characteristic figures – Europe's last chance, as it were, to produce a decent and suitably enlightened monarch before the French Revolution unleashed its furies.

Frederick had already fascinated a man whom Carlyle viewed with considerable distaste. Voltaire's *Memoirs of the Life of Monsieur de Voltaire* is curious for many reasons, not least because it is almost as much a *Life of Frederick the Great*. To say that the *philosophe* and the monarch had a love-hate relation would be an understatement on both counts. Voltaire wanted to make the king a philosopher; the king wanted Voltaire to make him a better poet (in French, of course, German being barely worth dignifying with his royal talents).

> The King of Prussia, to whom I had often intimated that I would never leave Mme du Châtelet for him, did his utmost to catch me now that he was rid of his rival. [She had just died.] At this time he was enjoying a period of peace that he had won through his victories, and his leisure time was always employed in writing poetry, or composing the history of his country and his campaigns. He was perfectly convinced, if truth be told, that his poetry and his prose were far better than my prose and my poetry, at least in content; but he believed that, when it came to form, I would, as an Academician, be able to impart a certain polish to his writings; there was no seductive flattery that he failed to employ in order to persuade me to come.

How could I resist a victorious king who was also a poet, musician and philosopher, and who claimed to love me? I thought that I loved him too. Eventually I set off for Potsdam in the month of June 1750.

The king gave him an apartment that had belonged to the Maréchal de Saxe; he could call on the services of the king's chefs and the king's coachmen; the dinners were delicious, and the talk at table was witty and relaxed. Voltaire spent two hours a day with His Majesty, correcting his poetry and discussing the finer points of rhetoric. He could not imagine a more delightful life – one in which he was free, with no visits to pay and only minimal duties. Frederick could see that his captive's head was turned, and

redoubled his magic potions to intoxicate me completely. The final act of seduction was a letter that he wrote from his apartment to me in mine. A mistress expresses her feelings no more tenderly; he endeavoured in this letter to dissipate the fear that his rank and his character inspired in me.

This was the last drop of magic potion, and Voltaire's cup was now filled to overflowing.

He was accustomed to making singular demonstrations of affection towards favourites who were younger than myself; and, forgetting for a moment that I was not their age, and that I did not have a pretty hand, he seized mine to kiss it. I kissed his in turn, and made myself his slave.

In this way did Monsieur de Voltaire make himself the servant of two masters, as he still needed to free himself from his bondage to the king of France. Permission from Louis was granted. Voltaire was now the servant of one master – or rather, the mistress. His memoirs are biography as a disappointed love story; an act of revenge in which the embers of passion still smoulder.

Carlyle is tart about Voltaire. His biography also, it is said, promotes Frederick as a king who imposed his will on Prussia, brought order out of chaos, overcame his weaknesses to forge a powerful identity for himself. '*Durchhalten!*' – 'hold on in there!' – was his motto and sustained Gustav von Aschenbach through many a weary vigil, not to mention being an inspiration for more dubious characters. But it is the *style* of his biography which keeps Frederick alive: any ideological message can be left safely to sink into the sands of Brandenburg.

Incidentally, Carlyle the biographer was also a biographee, of James Anthony Froude, who also wrote on the lives of Caesar, Erasmus, Luther, Bunyan, and Disraeli – a nice mixture of tempestuous and diplomatic souls. In his *Life of Carlyle*, Froude controversially laid bare some of the secrets of his marriage to Jane. When she had died, Carlyle read her diaries and wrote the 'Reminiscences of Jane Welsh Carlyle' as an act of remorse. He had been so obsessed with Frederick! Perhaps he should have left the dead to bury the dead? Virgina Woolf visited the house on Cheyne Walk on 24 February 1909. She wrote: 'There were portraits of Mrs Carlyle which seemed to look out quizzically upon the strangers as though they asked what they really found to look at: did they think that her house and her [sic] had been like that? Would she have tolerated them for a second?' But when you are dead, anyone can walk into your house quite unannounced, and read your private letters, even though you would have disdained even to give them the time of day.

Life of Napoleon

Chateaubriand's *Memoirs from Beyond the Grave* is an autobiography which, for a long section in the middle, becomes a biography of Napoleon, explicitly set out as such: 'I will follow the course of Bonaparte's great career, which nonetheless passed by so swiftly that his age occupies a brief part of the years covered by my *Memoirs*.' He even sees this as a duty rather than a pleasure: 'The fastidious reproduction of genealogies, the cold investigation of facts, and the dull verification of dates are duties to which the writer is constrained.' How does he enliven what does not seem an alluring task? By turning the 'Life of Napoleon' into a 'parallel life' of his own. Not that he sees the emperor as his alter ego; his view of the man, politically and in all sorts of other ways, was nuanced to say the least (and he offers other interesting and less egotistic parallels, casting the modest, 'democratic' Washington as the new man for a New World, while Napoleon is the last of the great European emperors). Rather, he counterpoints Bonaparte's life with his own. The result can be a little odd: of Napoleon's return from the Egyptian expedition, he notes, 'Napoleon takes the route I followed', as if the First Consul, hurrying back to France, had felt obliged to follow in the traces of his mighty predecessor. Or they can be poignant (the noise of the public realm versus the quieter events of the private: 'Bonaparte invades the Electorate of Hanover on June 3 [1803]: in Rome, I was then closing the eyes of a little-known woman [his mistress, the Comtesse de Beaumont]'). Or they can be moralising, like this sustained passage in which Chateaubriand, looking back on an earlier section of his auto-biography (which weaves backwards and forwards in time), reflects on the fates meted out to the two of them:

I told of my despondency and obscurity in London against the background of Napoleon's brilliant rise; the sound of his footsteps mingled with the silence of mine on my solitary walks; his name pursued me into those little rooms where were to be found the sad poverty of my companions in misfortune [...] Napoleon was my age: both of us left the womb of the army, and he won a hundred battles, while I still languished in the obscurity of the Emigration which was the pedestal of his fortune. Left so far behind, could I ever rejoin him? Nonetheless, while he was dictating the law to monarchs, while he was crushing their armies and making their blood spurt at his feet, while, flag in hand, he crossed the bridges at Arcola and Lodi, while he triumphed at the Pyramids, would I have given for all those victories a single one of those forgotten hours spent in England in a little unknown town? Oh, the magic of youth!

This antithesis, saturated with stock themes (Chateaubriand versus Bonaparte, happy obscurity versus tempestuous glory, etc.), sometimes gives way to identification:

The peace Napoleon concluded with kings and with his gaolers, he concluded with me also: I was a son of the sea as he was; my birthplace was a rock like his. I flatter myself that I understood Napoleon better than those who saw him more often and approached him more closely.

Both Chateaubriand and Napoleon were born in a rocky coastal town (Saint-Malo and Ajaccio respectively): *therefore*… In fact, this habit of plotting his own life against the lives of those who have gone before is like a constant cross-reference in Chateaubriand's *Memoirs*, which is a vast chamber of echoes. Like an internet browser (the tourist analogy is apt), he is always going off at a tangent. The result can be comically self-important or it can create a beautiful historical *sfumato* in which the past is brought back to tremulous life, or it can veer from one to the other. Discussing Napoleon's vexed relations with the Papacy, Chateaubriand mentions Pius VII leaving Rome by the Porta Pia.

This Porta Pia, where I have so often walked alone, was that by which Alaric entered Rome. Following the circuit along which Pius VII passed, I viewed the Villa Borghese as Raphael's retreat and Monte Pincio as the refuge of Claude

Lorrain and Poussin; marvellous memories of female beauty and the light of Rome; memories of artistic genius sponsored by Papal power, memories which might pursue and console a captive and despoiled prince.

What do the humiliations inflicted by Bonaparte matter to a man who holds spiritual as well as temporal power, and who can console himself with memories of the light of Rome, and its art?

Both Napoleon and Chateaubriand ended their earthly existence on rocky islands: the fallen emperor in St Helena, and the writer in the tomb he had arranged for himself on the Ile du Grand Bé, off Saint-Malo. Here Sartre came one day: he pissed on the tomb of this reactionary figure, and his piss trickled down into the tempestuous Atlantic waves. Chateaubriand, with his eery way of seeing all great men as alike, would not have minded too much: he would probably even have made a little parallel life out of it; for both men had consorted with the rulers of their day, Charles X here and Fidel Castro there; both had seen vast empires rise and fall; and both had been obsessed by the *Being and Nothingness* of human life.

Life of Nicholas II

Revisionist accounts of the lives of rulers are abundant, especially on the internet. A ruler is always, on one level, representative of his or her people, even if the latter were at times a little rebellious – in which case the ruler becomes representative of one side in an ideological civil war that may continue long after the real war has been lost and won. The life of the last of the tsars, for example, can be told in many ways. An account entitled 'The Royal Passion-Bearer and Martyr Nicholas Alexandrovich Romanov II' arouses certain expectations. They are not disappointed: this is not going to be a Marxist denunciation of a reactionary tyranny, or even a more sympathetic narrative of a man who, from the start of his reign, viewed his calling with such dread that he would burst into tears at his sense of unworthiness for it. We read:

Contrary to the popular, and widely taught, belief, Tsar Nicholas II cared for the Russian People. This is obvious when you look at his life – one filled with hardship. Not only was Russia discontent with the Tsar's rule, but the Tsarevich was afflicted with the rare disease haemophilia. All of this weighed heavily on the God-anointed Tsar, who desired more to become a monk, than to rule an empire.

Russia's 'discontent' with the Tsar's rule is obviously the fault of the former rather than the latter. And this biography has an axe to grind: it will set the record straight where so many other biographies have fallen prey to ideology.

Few figures in history have been so misunderstood and maligned as the Tsar-Martyr Nicholas II, the last emperor of Orthodox Holy Russia. The Modern 'Western' mind tends to view history in a strictly political way. But with an Orthodox world view, history must be seen as the unfolding of the story of man's redemption through the Incarnation of our Lord Jesus Christ, His death on the cross for our sakes, and His Holy Resurrection.

At least the paradigms by which this biography is being written are made clear. Critics of biographers often complain that they are being presented with a mass of ill-digested information, in which the key moments of a life are lost in a welter of irrelevancies, and its broken structure sinks, like the statue of Ozymandias, into the sands. Carlyle derided the Dryasdusts, the fact-obsessed who had smothered Frederick the Great and blurred his symbolic significance. No such problem here. Nicholas is a world-historical figure, but the world history in which, so to speak, the Tsar stars is not any which Hegel would have recognised. It is a world in which the very names of people and places cannot be stated in an unequivocally non-ideological way. Not just 'Nicholas II', but the 'Royal Passion-Bearer' and 'Martyr'; not just 'Russia' but 'Orthodox Holy Russia'.

> With the murder of Tsar Nicholas, the Byzantine form of government, which places Christ at its head, ended, ushering in the present age of lawlessness, apostasy and confusion. His was a government in the tradition begun sixteen centuries earlier by St. Constantine the Great. That such an unthinkable tragedy as the Russian Revolution could take place attests to the truth of the scriptural warning that 'because iniquity shall abound, the love of many shall wax cold' (Matt. 24:12). This pious Christian emperor was surrounded by people, even among his own relatives, whose self-centeredness and petty worldliness had obscured the love of God in their hearts to the point that they failed to unite around their sovereign in his time of need. They thereby cleared the way for the revolutionary element – the enemies of God – to despoil the Holy Russian Empire and place in its dead a satanocracy whose aim was the annihilation of the remembrance of God from the face of the earth.

It is difficult to imagine more being at stake: the life and death of Nicholas are part of a cosmic drama.

> Much has been written through the years about the tragedy of the Royal Martyrs – some well-meaning, some disappointingly critical, some outright slanderous – but almost none from the viewpoint of the Orthodox Christian 'measuring stick.' The life of Tsar-Martyr Nicholas must not be veiled in a political way if one wishes to see his life in its fullest.

So the biography continues, with the Tsar's birth and his up-bringing in 'Spartan simplicity' ('the Imperial palace at Gatchina had nine hundred rooms, but the Tsarevich and his siblings slept in army issue cots and had hard pillows. There were cold baths in the morning, and porridge for breakfast. These children were not spoiled as many would believe'). His coronation is a deliberate slap in the face for the West: 'A Tsar's coronation is always held in Moscow, not in the western capital of St. Petersburg, as the coronation of the Tsar is much too import-ant an event to be held in the modern world.' By this stage, the early rigours of life have been replaced with something a little more satisfying.

> The banquet meal consisted of borshch, pepper pot soup, turnovers filled with meat, steamed fish, young spring lamb, pheasants in cream sauce, salad, asparagus, sweet fruit, wine and ice cream. On a dais beneath a golden canopy, the Tsar and Tsaritsa dined. All that day the Tsar wore the enormous crown of Catherine the Great. It was so big it almost came over his eyes. Unfortunately it rested right over the scar made by his would-be Japanese assassin many years ago, giving him quite a headache.

Not enough biographers tell us what their subjects eat, but we are given full details here.

> During this time Christian literature flourished. Journals were published such as 'Soul-Profiting Reading', 'Russian Monk', and the ever-popular 'Russian Pilgrim'. Russia's people were surrounded with spiritual nourishment as they never before had been.

Is the biographer drawing a distinction here between 'spiritual nourishment' and the other kind? The People may not have enjoyed 'pheasants in cream sauce' all that often, but at least they could read – or have read to them – the 'Russian Pilgrim'. And yet sarcasm seems pretty ineffectual here; the biographer would probably just agree with me.

> More saints were glorified in Tsar Nicholas' reign than in that of any other Tsar. His love of Orthodoxy and the Church's holy ones was boundless. He often pressured the Holy Synod to make haste to glorify many of God's saints, including St. John (Maximovitch) of Tobolsk, the relative and patron of our modern St. John (Maximovitch) of Shanghai and San Francisco. St. Seraphim of Sarov was glorified at the Tsar's insistence in 1903. This is when Nicholas was made aware of the future apostasy and downfall of the Russian nation and the Church through a prophetic letter, to the Tsar, written by St. Seraphim himself. The Saint, shortly before his death in 1833, had written this letter and addressed it 'to the Tsar in whose reign I shall be glorified'. He then gave it to Elena Motovilov [who] kept the letter for seventy years and gave it to the Tsar at the glorification of St. Seraphim. The exact contents of the letter are unknown. Nevertheless, it is certain that St. Seraphim prepared the Tsar for the coming hardships.

So at least one evil omen is allowed to intrude on the early festive years. This biography does not mention another: the fact that, at the Tsar's coronation, there was a mass stampede which resulted in the crushing to death of scores of people.

This kind of biography is far from being a judicious appraisal of a complicated figure. Nor is it just an episode in the continuing Russian Civil War. It is a blow struck in a battle between good and evil. Of how many other biographies can this be said?

Part III
Parents and In-Laws

Life of Agricola

It used to be the practice to record the deeds and habits of famous men. Even our own time, though indifferent to its own children, has not abandoned the recording of great virtue. Tacitus begins his account of his father-in-law Julius Agricola with the usual denunciations of contemporary moral decadence, but he also points out the dangers of writing a biography. Before, good men could even publish their autobiographies without seeming pompous or self-serving; nowadays, even the eulogy of a man whose virtues seem to rebuke the current regime can be a capital offence. But at least, under Trajan, it should now be possible to publish the life story of Gnaeus Julius Agricola: such an exercise can always be excused by 'filial duty'.

Most of what we know about Agricola, apparently, we know from his son-in-law's biography. But since Agricola was largely responsible for pacifying the unruly tribes of Britain, where he was governor, a considerable proportion of Tacitus' narrative is taken up with that faraway, savage island, its southern parts shaped 'like a shield' or, some say, like a 'double-axe'. Agricola's life is the frame of a sustained piece of geographical and ethnographical writing: Tacitus dwells on the different characteristics of Silurians and Caledonians, of tribes of Iberian, Germanic or Gallic descendance. The sky is overcast; it is always cloudy and raining; but not too cold. Britain produces metals, gold and silver among them: it is a *pretium victoriae* ('well worth conquering'). The British have women as well as men rulers: Boudicca rebelled, and in her wrath of her victory omitted no sort of barbarian cruelty; but Paulinus, in a single battle, subdued the land to its earlier docility (*patientiae*). When Agricola lost his one-year-old son, he did not react with a show of stoicism, nor with the weeping and wailing of a woman; instead, he consoled himself by fighting, and in AD 83 or 84 launched an attack at Mons Graupius, somewhere in the north-eastern Highlands, where he was met by an army of 30,000 Caledonians, led by Calgacus. Tacitus gives him a stirring speech. 'Here,' he tells the troops, 'there is a leader, an army: there, taxes and metal and the other torments of slavery.' By 'metal' (*metalla*) he meant 'labour in the mines'.

The Caledonians were beaten. The speech seems to have been an invention of Tacitus'; it is not even certain that Calgacus existed outside this text. He was, no doubt, the kind of Caledonian chief who did exist, and some of the words attributed to him by Tacitus are among those most remembered by that fierce, terse writer, whose name seems so apt (elliptical, economical, tight-lipped to the point of silence). Tacitus gives Calgacus a biting denunciation of Roman imperialism: they overrun the world, are satisfied by neither East nor West, alone of mankind plunder rich and poor with equal avarice. 'Plundering butchering stealing – this is their so-called "empire", and where they spread desolation, they call it "peace" [*atque ubi solitudinem faciunt, pacem appellant*].'

Agricola died in his bed, in retirement in Gaul. If there is any place where the spirits of the just go after death, may he rest in peace there, says Tacitus, who, in the middle of this biography, has nonetheless inserted a striking vignette of other lives brought under the *imperium* of the Roman people, and ventriloquised through them a passionate denunciation of what that same *imperium* meant.

Yes, but which one? Philip Henry Gosse (1810–88) was a marine biologist, whose work *Omphalos* attempted to demonstrate that the vast geological epochs laid open by contemporary geology could in fact be reconciled with the idea of divine creation *ex nihilo*: on one reading, he was implying that God planted fossils in the rocks (so that they were not in fact traces of extinct life-forms that had evolved over millions of years); he was certainly struggling to articulate the way in which time often seems to be a human invention, playing little part in the real world revealed to us by science, the Scriptures, etc. *Omphalos* was greeted with perplexity, scepticism, and some distaste.

Edmund Gosse (1849–1928) was his son, a highly successful writer in many genres, and a well-known biographer, mainly of other writers – Donne and Congreve, Jeremy Taylor and Swinburne, Thomas Browne and Thomas Gray. He was interested in the less orthodox aspects of some of his biographees: his *Confidential Paper on Swinburne's Moral Irregularities* was for a long time kept in the 'reserved from public use' section of the British Museum Reading Room (what the French call the *enfer* of a library). He also wrote a biography of his father, *The Life of Philip Henry Gosse, FRS*. As the title suggests, it was rather a formal affair, an act of filial piety. (PHG had circulated *A Memorial of the Last Days on Earth of Emily Gosse*, his wife, who died when Edmund was just a boy. This was an act of uxorious piety; as its title suggests, the grief of Gosse *père* was partly mitigated by the belief that *days on earth* are not all.) George Moore, on reading the biography of the FRS, thought that it contained the germ of something more exciting: in 1907, anonymously, Gosse *fils* published *Father and Son*. This focused less on his father's scientific speculations than on his shortcomings as a father: bigoted, repressive, joyless PHG, a member of the Plymouth Brethren, had attempted to turn EG into one of the 'Saints'. Young Gosse struggled to maintain the faith but – as was the case for Charles

Darwin – was repelled by the doctrine of eternal punishment, in which (*see* Dante) one is trapped in one's biography forever and ever. Edmund read Shakespeare and Keats, and – with less fervour – Shelley and Wordsworth. He read the Bible *for himself* – a crucial step on the road to true emancipation. He started to realise just how narrow a world his father lived in. Not a single Unitarian could be redeemed, let alone Catholics. Interestingly, the elder Gosse 'thought that the ordinary Chinaman or savage native of Fiji had a better chance of salvation than any cardinal in the Vatican. And even in the priesthood of the Church of England he believed that while many were called, few indeed would be found to have been chosen.' Ideological war between father and son was inevitable. Edmund Gosse's account ends in a cry of triumph:

> No compromise, it is seen, was offered; no proposal of a truce would have been acceptable. It was a case of 'Everything or Nothing'; and thus desperately challenged, the young man's conscience threw off once and for all the yoke of his 'dedication', and, as respectfully as he could, without parade or remonstrance, he took a human being's privilege to fashion his inner life for himself.

It was the time (it always is) for young men to turn against their fathers. But there is something odd about the way that, just as he achieves independent self-hood, the 'I' of the narrative suddenly becomes a 'he', and falls prey to uncertain cliché and a bizarrely stilted formality. In her dual biography of father and son, Ann Twaite shows how the 'scrupulously true' *Father and Son* was not, and how EG traduced his father. Her work is called *Glimpses of the Wonderful*: it is not just a contribution to a dull, Oedipal squabble, but releases both men into something indeed wonderful.

A few years later, another rebellious young man would displace family, race, and religion, and rewrite patriarchy, more subtly, but with even greater fervour: Stephen Dedalus, daring to be Icarus, taking leave of and with his 'old father, old artificer'. A little later, Sigmund Freud would have his disturbance of memory on the Acropolis, and realise that he had got to where his father never had, and that he missed old Jakob – for now he, too, was an old man.

Omphalos, by Philip Henry Gosse, is still read and admired for the grimly tenacious splendour with which it pursues a massively counter-intuitive but possibly undisprovable hypothesis.

Life of Ackerley

'I am not going to make any excuses, old man. I have done my duty towards everybody as far as my nature would allow and I hope people generally will be kind to my memory. All my men pals know of my second family and of their mother, so you won't find it difficult to get on their track.' These words were left by Roger Ackerley to his son, J.R. Ackerley, the writer (and editor of *The Listener*), in a sealed envelope. Roger had just died (of tertiary syphilis); what JRA discovered was that he had fathered three daughters by another woman (Muriel Perry) and kept this secret from his 'official' family (and from his daughters, who thought he was their Uncle Bodger). The bluff term 'old man', addressed here from dead father to living son, as from one pal to another, is interesting: the father knew as little of the son's homosexuality as the son had known of the father's other family.

J.R. Ackerley's *My Father and Myself* is a parallel life, or even a mirrored double life. His father was the opposite of Gosse senior: an easy-going man, who intervened little in family life, and over port and cigars with JRA would soon reach 'an unbuttoned stage of mellowness and ease', and regale him with tales of his huge sexual appetite, and told his sons that 'in the matter of sex there was nothing he had not done, no experience he had not tasted, no scrape he had not got into and out of' – as when he was almost caught '*in flagrante delicto* with his colour-sergeant's young wife'. JRA wondered whether his father may even have been drawn to the guardsmen with whom he had served in the army, before making money as 'The Banana King of London'. If so, JRA had inherited the taste, with a vengeance: after his teddy bear, guardsmen were one of the son's primary erotic obsessions. This remains speculative, but the respective secrets of Roger and JRA bind them together in the latter's (auto)biography. 'Like father, like son': truest when most ironic.

When one of the daughters, Diana Petre, wrote her autobiography in 1975, she called it *The Secret Orchard of Roger Ackerley* – the term 'secret orchard' again coming from one of Roger's letters.

Use the enemy's strength against him: one lesson to be learnt from biographers.

Life of Henriette Barthes

The last book by Roland Barthes, *Camera Lucida*, was ostensibly about photography. It was also a biography of his mother, Henriette Barthes, who had just died. 'A biography? But we learn hardly anything about her!' We learn as much as we need to, no? Barthes rigorously controls the amount of information he will vouchsafe us; though this is a book about photography, it is also a book about the *one* photograph that captured his mother's 'essence' for him, discovered only when she was dead – and it is a photograph of her from when she was a little girl, long before RB himself had known her (and of course he refuses to show it to us, since it would be of only vague cultural interest). From this photograph he derives an essence that transcends time, and on this basis decides that the essence of photography it that it also transcends time, albeit in a peculiarly painful way, preserving for us now what is always a *past* moment. In this way the art of photography and the art of biography become interwoven. Barthes is as discreet as ever; out he comes with his polite theory, but the groans of grief are all the more poignant.

Defining a genre is of little interest: testing it to destruction is much more revealing. Many of the best biographies are a bit monstrous and maniacal (Carlyle's *Frederick the Great*), or else they are modest and even minimal (*Camera Lucida*). Henriette Barthes becomes the (silent) author of her son's days. Of course she had another life (we do in fact glimpse her, or so it seems, at the beginning of *Roland Barthes by Roland Barthes*, but the photo is hazy; widowed young, she led an impecunious life as a bookbinder in Paris, produced another son – Barthes's half-brother – out of wedlock, etc.). But everyone has another life.

There are successful biographies that are little more than photo albums. (Lives can also be sung, danced, drawn, painted, sculpted, filmed, acted out, etc.; indeed, they are increasingly being emailed, youtubed, tweeted, facebooked, in various melds and merges, fusions and crossovers, of bio- and autobiography. All singing! All dancing!)

Part IV
Philosophers, Mathematicians and Scientists

Life of Socrates

The loss of so many of the works of Antiquity is a matter for regret (and relief). This is especially true in the case of Aristoxenus of Tarentum, who was active c. 330 BC. He learned music from his accomplished father and was, according to the great anecdotalist Aulus Gellius, instructed by the Pythagorean Xenophilus in the tenets of the Master. (Both pseudo-Lucian and Pliny tell us that this Xenophilus lived to the age of 105 without a single day's sickness – perhaps because of his avoidance of beans.) Aristoxenus became a student of Aristotle and, inspired by the latter, built up a store of polymathic erudition. After Aristotle's death, Aristoxenus either heaped scorn and insult on his memory, since Aristotle had named Theophrastus as head of his school, the Lyceum, or he continued to revere his teacher's memory and promote his programme of research (accounts differ). He wrote 453 books: three books of a treatise on music have survived. (He thought that the soul was a harmony between the four elements of the body. On the dissolution of the latter, the harmony too vanished into silence – a theme recently explored, with picturesque inconsequentiality, in *Le Quattro Volte*.)

Among his myriad other interests, Aristoxenus was a biographer of philosophers. He wrote the lives of Pythagoras and other Pythagoreans, including Archytas of Tarentum (who, some have said, inspired Plato with the idea of the philosopher king and, according – again – to Aulus Gellius, invented a kind of flying machine, called 'The Dove', apparently propelled by steam). Aristoxenus also wrote lives of Socrates and Plato: the fragments that have come down to us are very impolite. For example, he claims that for all the brilliant cultural life on offer around him, Socrates remained a boorish, uncouth character.

The life of Socrates can also be reassembled from the dialogues of Plato and Xenophon, and the (much later) account by Diogenes Laertius. But what if Aristoxenus' account casts a shadow over all of them? What if he brings out aspects of Socrates that they conceal, or of which they were simply unaware? Is the idea of a 'definitive' biography not simply a contradiction in terms?

Life of Descartes

In Adrien Baillet's *Life of Monsieur Descartes*, we are informed that, on 10 November 1619, Descartes,

having gone to bed *quite filled with his inspiration [enthousiasme]*, and overwhelmed at the idea *that he had, on this day, discovered the foundations of the admirable science*, he had three consecutive dreams, that were so extraordinary that he imagined they might have come to him from above. He thought that he could discern, through their shadows, the vestiges of the path which God was tracing out for him to follow his will in his choice of life, and in the quest for that truth about which he was so anxious. But the spiritual and divine air that he affected to give to the explanations he gave of his dreams was so influenced by the inspiration that had set him on fire, that one would have been inclined to think that his brain was weakened, or that he had been drinking the evening before he went to sleep.

And indeed, it was the eve of Saint Martin's day, on the evening of which it was customary to have wild parties in the place where he was [Germany], as in France. But he assures us that he had spent the evening and the whole day in great soberness, and that he had not drunk wine for a full three months.

This excerpt reports on one of the turning points, not just of the life of Descartes, but of the history of philosophy. Descartes himself relates it in his *Discourse on the Method*: it was during the winter break in the Thirty Years War that he shut himself away in a stove-heated room and struggled with the problem of how to establish some firm base for philosophising. He notes his dreams (we have fuller access to them from other accounts he left: dreams, those crucial moments in a person's life, are accessible to others, if at all, *only* through that person's report). What he concluded was the Cogito, the birth of the modern subject. This subject transcends the material world; it cannot be captured by any biography. And yet, in the *Discourse*, Descartes chose to narrate this discovery as part of his life story, and invited his readers to meditate so that, following the path he had taken, they too might be free of their biographies. The best life was hidden, thought Descartes.

Life of Heidegger

Heidegger wrote of Aristotle: 'he lived, he thought, he died'. That was all the biography a philosopher needed. All the rest was 'anecdote'.

Someone once said to Heidegger, 'What about the gospels? Aren't they all just anecdotes, too?'

Heidegger did not answer.[17]

Life of Pierre de Fermat

'No three positive integers a, b, and c can satisfy the equation an + bn = cn for any integer value of n greater than two.'

Life of Andrew Wiles

'No three positive integers a, b, and c can satisfy the equation an + bn = cn for any integer value of n greater than two. […] QED.'

Life of Kepler

One of the finest 'group' biographies of scientists is Arthur Koestler's *The Sleepwalkers*, which details the struggle of astronomers in the early modern period to make the great breakthrough out of the Ptolemaic system. Koestler is harsh on Copernicus, the 'timid canon', and a little dry on Galileo. (Brecht redressed the balance in his *Life of Galileo*.) But Koestler's imagination is, quite understandably, fired by Kepler, who straddled the medieval and modern worlds, drawn as much to alchemy and palmistry and the music of the spheres as to the dictates of mathematics and superior conjunctions. As he lay dying, Kepler had lost the power of speech. He kept pointing, first to his forehead, then upwards to the skies. But nobody knew what he meant.

Life of Darwin

There is a fine life of Darwin by Ruth Padel (*Darwin. A Life in Poems*, 2009). There is no reason for biography to be an essentially prosaic genre.

Part V
Musicians and Writers

Life of Mozart

First, Mozart was deified. These days, he is *Amadeified*.

Life of Beethoven

The death of Beethoven was a dramatic event fully in keeping with the tenor of his life. It was orchestrated by crashes of thunder worthy of the kettledrums of the *Eroica* or the Fifth Symphony – at least in the written accounts that have come down to us.

Professor Dr Andreas Johann Wawruch was Beethoven's last physician. He attended the now stone-deaf composer almost every day during his final illness, communicating with him by writing his instructions on a sheet of paper. He advised Beethoven to ask for the ministrations of a priest. As did other witnesses, Wawruch reports that, after his piously performed 'devotions', and once the priest had gone, Beethoven said to his friends, '*Plaudite amici, comoedia finite est!*' This was the phrase which concluded Latin dramas; the word *comoedia* may mean 'play', rather than comedy; Beethoven may have been referring to the sacrament of extreme unction (he was not above gruff jokes about even his most heartfelt beliefs) or about his whole life, dismissed or celebrated in Shakespearian terms as a play.

Anselm Hüttenbrenner was from Graz in Austria, a student of Salieri, a composer, and a friend of Schubert. (It was to Hüttenbrenner that Schubert sent the manuscript of his Unfinished Symphony, around 1823.) His C minor Requiem was performed at Schubert's funeral in December 1828. Barely eighteen months before, he had visited Beethoven on his death bed with several other people, including 'Professor Schindler'; the rest of the company, however, left, so that when Beethoven died, only Hüttenbrenner and Frau van Beethoven (presumably the widow of Beethoven's brother – the woman whom Beethoven had nicknamed the 'Queen of the Night') were with him.

Hüttenbrenner described the scene of the afternoon of 26 March 1827:

Beethoven lay in his final agony, unconscious, and with the death-rattle in his throat, from 3 o'clock, when I arrived, to after five. There was a sudden, loud clap of thunder, together with a bolt of lightning, illuminating the death chamber with a harsh light (there was snow lying outside Beethoven's house). After this unforeseen natural phenomenon, which had greatly perturbed me, Beethoven opened his eyes, lifted his right hand, and, with his fist clenched, looked upwards for several seconds with a very serious, threatening expression, as if saying, 'I defy you, powers of evil! Away! God is with me.' It was also as if he were calling, like a valiant commander to his faint-hearted troops, 'Courage, men! Forward! Trust in me! Victory is ours!'

As he let his hand fall back onto the bed, his eyes half closed. My right hand lay under his head, and my left rested on his chest. He had stopped breathing, his heart had ceased to beat! The spirit of the great composer fled from this world of deception into the kingdom of truth. I shut the dead man's half-closed eyes, kissed them and then his forehead, mouth and hands. At my request, Frau van Beethoven cut off a lock of his hair and gave it to me as a sacred relic of Beethoven's last hour.

This account was not in fact published until over forty years later, in the Graz *Tagespost* of 23 October 1868. By this stage, Hüttenbrenner had been a follower of a man called Jakob Lorber for nearly twenty years, and had helped him to transcribe the words dictated to him by his inner voice (or Jesus Christ).

And as for this lock of hair, its fate is narrated in *Beethoven's Hair* by Russell Martin: a tale involving terrors even greater than those claps of thunder against which Beethoven apparently shook his dying fist. Like all relics, it is a bit of the dead person that assumes an uncanny life (life-in-death) all of its own, as a fetish – not unlike the works of art left over from the creative life.

There are several biopics about Beethoven; perhaps unfortunately they tend to focus on the 'Immortal Beloved', as in the film of that name. This is not true of *Beethoven Lives Upstairs*, which sees a period in the composer's life through the eyes of Christoph, a young Viennese boy whose mother rents out the room upstairs to a shabby, eccentric, half-deaf figure. The story is told in retrospect, based on the letters which Christoph had written to his uncle about the stroppy, scary, sudden man who writes music. The film is one of a series produced in Canada (others include *Mr Bach Comes to Call*, *Mozart's Magical Adventure*, *Tchaikovsky Discovers America*, and so on). It stars Neil Munro as Beethoven, and includes a part for Beethoven's notoriously unreliable biographer, Anton Schindler.

Beethoven's music is often rooted in his life (the panic attack in the first movement of the Second Symphony, composed at the time when he realised his deafness was increasing). But music plots life differently. The hero (if there is one) in the *Eroica* is already dead by the time the second movement begins. And when the main 'Creatures of Prometheus' theme of the finale is played *backwards*, we are in a realm far beyond heroes, whether Napoleon or even Beethoven.

(Several films called *Beethoven* are not really about the composer at all.)

Life of Glenn Gould

He had a fascinating life, of course, and there are some excellent biographies of him. But, despite his claim that he did not practice much, he did spend a lot of his life playing the piano, alone. And this is the condition of possibility for everything else.

The truly inspiring biopics show the writer or composer just writing, the musician practising, the painter making marks on a piece of canvas...

Life of Carrie Fisher

In the early 1980s, Paul Simon had a stormy liaison (is there ever any other kind?) with actress Carrie Fisher, whom he had met in 1978. She was from the west coast, he from New York; as so often, their love affair was a marriage of sea with shining sea. They were married, briefly, in 1983. She suffered from substance abuse and what these days would be called 'bipolar disorder'.

Simon has been hailed as a literate and confessional songwriter. He has been spurred into song by, among other things, three break-ups with people close to him (three real or symbolic 'divorces'). The split with his first wife, Peggy Harper, gave rise to 'Train in the Distance'. The dissolution of his artistic partnership with Art Garfunkel produced 'So long Frank Lloyd Wright'. And his divorce from Carrie Fisher was echoed in 'Hearts and Bones' (1983). Here is a biographical event that was transfigured by art – at least, that is one way of putting it. The degree to which we understand the song better when we know of the life story behind it is a moot (and rather boring) point. Nonetheless, it is a feature of contemporary cultural life that the 'real story' behind the music should often be a source of fascination. In *The Girl in the Song: The Real Stories Behind 50 Classic Pop Songs*, by Michael Heatley and Frank Hopkinson (2010), we are given the biographical circumstances behind some of the chart-toppers of recent years, including the genesis of 'Hearts and Bones' (which sold poorly on release; these were the days before the triumph of *Graceland*). We also read that the woman 'behind' the song had a life after it. 'Carrie Fisher has survived drugs and depression to become a successful author. She has published fictionalised accounts of her dependencies (*Postcards from the Edge*) and her relationship with Paul (*Surrender the Pink*), while an autobiography, *Wishful Drinking*, has now become a successful one-woman stage show.' In the show she admits to finding it 'trippy' to hear songs on the radio about a relationship that ended over twenty-five years ago.

Life of Milton

Samuel Johnson's biography on Milton in *Lives of the English Poets* contains some well-known remarks. William Hayley's later biography is an anti-biography, or rather an anti-Johnson. Hayley, the friend and patron of Blake, wrote that Johnson's *Lives* 'will probably give birth, in this or the next century, to a work of literary retaliation. Whenever a poet rises with as large a portion of spleen towards the critical writers of past ages, as Johnson indulged towards the poets in his poetical autobiography, the literature of England will be enriched with "the Lives of the Critics".' He writes:

In emulation of that spirit, which delights to honour the excellencies of an illustrious antagonist, I have endeavoured to preserve in my own mind, and to express on every proper occasion, my unshaken regard for the rare faculties and virtues of a late extraordinary biographer, whom it has been my lot to encounter continually as a very bitter, and sometimes, I think, an insidious enemy to the great poet, whose memory I have fervently wished to rescue from indignity and detraction.

Johnson's 'asperity', he says, sometimes excites laughter, sometimes indignation among 'the fond admirers of the poet'. Addressing the dedicatee of his biography, Warton, Hayley writes:

You, my dear Warton [...] have heard the harsh critic advance in conversation an opinion against Milton, even more severe than the detractive sarcasms with which his life of the great poet abounds; you have heard him declaim against the admiration excited by the poetry of Milton, and affirm it to be nothing more than the cant (to use his own favourite phrase) of affected sensibility.

Johnson had been 'insidious' to Milton outside his biography, too. In his *Dictionary*, under the headword 'Sonnet', he cited the line 'A book was writ of late called Tetrachordon'. This, says Hayley, was surely the very sonnet that would have been adduced in evidence by an enemy wishing to cast 'scorn and derision' on Milton. Perhaps – he adds, more charitably – Johnson (who was not so fond of sonnets) was simply trying to deter young poets from attempting a verse form in which even the great poet had failed.

There is evidence for this view in Boswell's *Life of Johnson*. Aged seventy-five, Johnson and Boswell paid a visit to Oxford, which Boswell calls 'that magnificent and venerable seat of

Learning, Orthodoxy, and Toryism'. (It is still, indeed, a great seat of learning.) They spent a very pleasant time in the Master's Lodge of Pembroke, Johnson's old college, 'without restraint, and with superiour [sic] elegance', with the company of ladies. 'Mrs Kennicot related, in his [the Master's, I think] presence, a lively saying of Dr. Johnson to Miss Hannah More, who had expressed a wonder that the poet who had written *Paradise Lost* should write such poor Sonnets: – "Milton, Madam, was a genius that could cut a Colossus from a rock; but could not carve heads upon cherry-stones".'

Behind these aesthetic considerations lie political issues. The English have never warmed to Milton: this regicide reminds them too much of the English Civil War, and biographies of him always have to take sides in that continuing struggle.

Life of Coleridge

I was now back in London, in a flat below Highgate Hill. The figure of Coleridge […] was walking slowly down that hill, at what Keats called 'his alderman after-dinner pace', towards me. I often wandered over Hampstead Heath, up the small lane 'by Lord Mansfield's house' where Coleridge met Keats one spring afternoon in 1819, and talked of poetry, dreams, monsters, and nightingales. I longed to join in that conversation, and hear Coleridge's voice myself. Instead I stood silently under the chestnut trees outside No 3 The Grove, and looked up at the third-floor study where he had spent the last decade of his life, watching for any encouraging movement at the window. Very frequently, it seemed to start raining.

– Richard Holmes, *Sidetracks*

The ghost refuses to appear, and the rain (real? imaginary?) adds a plangent tone of melancholy. But:

Later I found that Coleridge's room in fact looked out over the garden, at the back, where he wrote many of his last poems, and this was a lesson in the presumption of the biographer who assumes he can step like a tourist into the past.

So of Coleridge it can be said, 'he is not here': the spirit of place is displaced, there is nothing to be seen at the site of imagination. The biographer here is cast as a stalker (as Charles Kinbote stalks John Shade in *Pale Fire*), or even Swann in love trying to surprise Odette and hanging around, consumed by jealousy and longing, outside her window (but it isn't).

Life of Baudelaire

When Charles Baudelaire was arrested for his offence against public morals (*Les Fleurs du Mal*), he was sitting peacefully in the cemetery of Montparnasse, reading Boswell's *Life of Johnson*.

Life of Jules Michelet

Barthes on Michelet: 'In this little book, the reader will find neither a history of Michelet's thought, nor a history of his life, and even less an explanation of the one by the other.' His task has been to 'discover the structure of an existence (I am not saying: of a life), a thematics, if you like, or rather: an organised network of obsessions. The real critiques can come later, historical or psychoanalytical (Freudian, Bachelardian or existential), this is merely a pre-critique: I have sought merely to describe a unity, and not to explore its roots in history or in biography.' The 'Memento' at the beginning gives the entry on Michelet from the *Petit Larousse Illustré, 1906–1934*; a chronology of Michelet's life that consists simply of two sentences by Michelet himself ('I was born during the great territorial revolution and I will have seen the hatching [*poindre*] of the great industrial revolution. Born under the terror of Babeuf, I am witnessing before my death the terror of the International'); there is a brief list of his forebears, his studies, the stages in his career, the influences on him, his love affairs, the tenets of his 'ideology', and his works. This is supplemented, at the end of the volume, by a fuller but dryer chronological overview, which, seeing Michelet as *essentially* the writer of the *History of the French Revolution*, divides his life into BEFORE, DURING and AFTER this event.

Michelet's illness is migraine; it can be provoked by the weather, or by the history he is narrating. The revolutionary events of September 1792 – the start of the Convention and the Terror – bring on a 'historical' (but just as real) migraine.

Michelet has a way of evaluating people in terms of his own physiology. Napoleon, continuer or betrayer of the Revolution? More important – or inseparable from his political impact – is his body: his eyes are grey or black, his skin yellow and waxy-white, he has no eyebrows. Marie-Louise, given to him in marriage, was like a fresh and pink-cheeked virgin, a 'rose' being delivered to 'the Minotaur'.

Michelet viewed history as a resurrection (the words on his tomb). The historian is a magistrate charged with the care of the dead.

Never in my career have I lost from sight this duty of the Historian. I have given to many of the dead who have been unjustly forgotten the assistance that I myself will need. [...] History welcomes and renews these disinherited glories [*ces gloires désheritées*]; it gives life to these dead, resurrects them. Its justice thus brings together those who did not live at the same time, enacts reparation to many who had appeared for only a brief moment only to disappear.

They now live with us, and we feel that we are their rela-
tives, their friends. In this way a family comes into being,
a shared city for both the living and the dead.

– *History of the Nineteenth Century*

Life of Mallarmé

Mallarmé: 'The pure work implies the elocutionary disappear-
ance of the poet, who leaves the initiative to words.' Writing
in 1885 to Verlaine, who had asked for some brief details of
his life to preface his poems, he described his life as 'devoid
of anecdote'.

Life of Tolstoy

On the '*Grande Levée*' of Tolstoy's grandfather, Prince Nicholas
Sergeyevich Tolstoy:

> And when the double doors of the dressing-room swung
> open at last, there was not one among the assembly who
> did not feel something akin to fear at the sight of the little,
> withered old man tottering stiffly towards him out of the
> depths of the ages, in a powdered wig above heavy black
> brows that shaded an expression of sparkling youth.
> – Henri Troyat, *Tolstoy*, translated by Nancy Amphoux (1967).

On the morning appearance of Prince Nicholas Andreyevich
Bolkonsky:

> Everyone sitting in this antechamber experienced the same
> feeling of respect and even fear when the enormously high
> study door opened and showed the figure of a rather small
> old man, with powdered wig, small withered hands, and

bushy gray eyebrows which, when he frowned, sometimes hid the gleam of his shrewd, youthfully glittering eyes.

– Tolstoy, *War and Peace*, translated by Aylmer Maude.

Life of Alice B. Toklas

The Autobiography of Alice B. Toklas tells of how Alice B. Toklas was born into a family in San Francisco, USA, where there was a great fire and she met the mother of Gertrude Stein and moved to Paris, France, in 1907. There she ran a household with Gertrude Stein, and Gertrude Stein's housemaid Helene was a very good housemaid, and Picasso and his mistress Fernande came round frequently. But Picasso broke up with Fernande, who moved to Montparnasse and taught French, so Gertrude visited her there, with Alice. Gertrude's brother Leo Stein bought paintings by Cézanne and Matisse from Ambroise Vollard, whose picture Cézanne had painted, and they were all friends and had a gay time, and Gertrude Stein was also friends with Apollinaire but then they broke up. Gertrude Stein was born in Alleghany, Pennsylvania, and then she lived in New York City and California and studied at Radcliffe College, and she was taught by William James, but she started a Masters at Johns Hopkins and was bored, and lived in London, and America, and Paris. Gertrude Stein went on holiday in Italy and Spain, with Alice. There was a war and Gertrude Stein drove round Paris with Alice to help the wounded. After the war Paris seemed changed, and Gertrude Stein quarrelled with T.S. Eliot, but made friends with Ernest Hemingway. Gertrude Stein was interested in this thing of reading about herself in the autobiography of Alice B. Toklas, but others were not, because they said that Alice should have written more about herself and her cooking.

Reactions to Toklas' autobiography were varied. Carl van Hechten liked the autobiography, but Ernest Hemingway said it was a damned pitiful book, and Monsieur Matisse thought it did not show Madame Matisse in a good light, and Georges Braque said it did not understand cubism which was so important for Gertrude Stein, and Alice, and Leo Stein thought it was a farrago of lies, and Gertrude Stein quarrelled with Ernest Hemingway, Henri Matisse, Georges Braque, and Leo Stein, but about the book, not always about other things, and Gertrude Stein had some more gay parties with artists and writers, and Alice.

Yes, it is easy to produce a (dreadful) pastiche of Gertrude Stein. It is slightly more interesting to dwell, as so many others have, on the odd *chasse-croisé* of this 'autobiography'. Although Stein is using Toklas as a ventriloquist's dummy, the book, it has been claimed, really *is* Toklas'. What may seem to be a hilarious act of literary hijacking may reflect a loving relationship in which the boundary between the two people is constantly becoming permeable.

Is it really possible to write the life of Morecambe without Wise? Of Tom without Jerry? Of Laurel without Hardy? Of Bouvard without Pécuchet? 'But there is an asymmetry here' – they will say. 'Stein wrote and Toklas did not.' But discursive power does not always reside with the writer. Perhaps Stein wrote *selon* Toklas. And in any case, Toklas *did* write. She wrote a cookbook. And an autobiography, too. It ends with the death of Gertrude Stein.

Life of Virginia Woolf

The preface to Woolf's *Orlando: A Biography* thanks for their help people who were never actually consulted. Sinologist Arthur Waley did not give a hand with Chinese, nor did Madame Lopokova (Mrs J.M. Keynes) provide assistance with Russian. 'Miss M.K. Snowdon's indefatigable researches in the archives of Harrogate and Cheltenham were none the less arduous for being vain.'

In a less facetious guise, Woolf, as Orlando's biographer, deploys many of the tropes of the genre. There is the (feigned, or hypocritical) acknowledgement that the biographee is not always a nice person so maybe we should be tactful about any misdemeanours: looking at the young Orlando, 'we have to admit a thousand disagreeables which it is the aim of every good biographer to ignore'. (She may be being ironic, of course.) There is the hypothetical question attributed to one of the characters: when Elizabeth (Queen) looks at Orlando, we read: 'Was she matching her speculations the other night with the truth now visible? Did she find her guesses justified?' There is the oft-repeated note that the biographer is often dependent on gossip, for 'so tradition has it'. There is the local colour: '[Orlando] had thrust on crimson breeches, lace collar, waist-coat of taffeta, and shoes with rosettes on them as big as double dahlias in less than ten minutes by the stable clock' (the biographer here, in an audacious moment of what narratologists call 'focalisation', skilfully adopts her subject's point of view). There is the topos that *it was all so long ago*, so that the very language in which the biographer discusses her subject is grossly 'belated', untimely. The very attempt to respect the otherness of the past betrays it, while the insistence that the past is a foreign country surreptitiously slips the passport to it into our hands: 'The age was Elizabethan; their morals were not ours; not their poets; nor their climates; nor their vegetables even. Everything was different.'

There is the topos for which no technical term, as far as I know, has yet been invented; this manoeuvre acknowledges the impossibility of recapturing a past moment and so indulges in flagrant anachronism: 'After an hour or so – the sun was rapidly sinking, the white clouds had turned red, the hills were violet, the woods purple, the valleys black – a trumpet sounded. Orlando leapt to his feet'. Yes, and he has obviously recently seen an exhibition of early canvases by Malevich, Kandinsky and the Fauves (we can call this topos the biographer's 'might-as-well-be-hanged-for-a-sheep-as-for-a-lamb'). There is the coy supposition, the biographer's joy and bane: 'perhaps'. There is the cautious indication of hereditary traits: 'Here, indeed, we lay bare rudely, as a biographer may, a curious trait in him, to be accounted for, perhaps [!], by the fact that a certain grandmother of his had worn a smock and carried milkpails. Some grains of the Kentish or Sussex earth [spirit of place, crucial in anyone's life story] were mixed with the thin, fine fluid which came to him from Normandy' – which explains Orlando's 'liking for low company'. There is the ascription of direct speech to the biographee when all the biographer really knows is that he may have said, or thought, this kind of thing: this is the biographer giving the biographee a helping hand (as happens these days in the writing up of interviews, the editorial clean-ups in Hansard, etc.[18]): '"All ends in death," Orlando would say, sitting upright, his face clouded with gloom. (For that was the way his mind worked now, in violent see-saws from life to death, stopping at nothing in between, so that the biographer must not stop either, but must fly as fast as he can and so keep pace with the unthinking passionate foolish actions and sudden extravagant words in which, it is impossible to deny, Orlando at this time of life indulged.)' There is the doublethink about the impermeability of other languages (the language(s) in which a biography is written haul the biographee into radically different universes, of startling strangeness, as anyone who has read one of the – very fine – biographies of Virginia Woolf in French will know): Woolf has initially reported verbatim the French of the Muscovite princess whom Orlando nicknames Sasha, but then grows shy about Sasha's witty comments to Orlando, all of which were in French, 'which notoriously loses its flavour in translation' (but which she omits to give us in French, no doubt in case she fails to be witty).[19] There is the importing of flagrantly private concerns that really have no place here (the whole biography keeps alluding to its dedicatee, Vita Sackville-West, who (like Orlando) spoke French with a perfect accent, had a head gardener called Stubbs, etc.). How many other biographers slip their private desires and obsessions into somebody else's life story? There is the need to show the biographee among other historical personages: he may be an episode in their lives, they are an episode in his: we are footnotes in each other's biographies. Elizabeth I and gentle Shakespeare drift like brief ghosts through this biography. More concretely, we see Pope: our expectations are aroused; it will be good to have an acerbic couplet or two after the gorgeous but fusty Elizabethan brocades. But we are not permitted to hear him at his best. His talk is as small as the rest, until he decides to let fly – whereupon the company is appalled: '"Mr Pope," said old Lady R. in a voice trembling with sarcastic fury, "you are pleased to be witty". Mr. Poe flushed red. Nobody spoke a word. They sat in dead silence some twenty minutes.' There is, finally, the hyping of the biographee's ultimate unknowability. Orlando is disgraced, retires to the country, and falls asleep for a week. When he awakens, he is a different person. This metamorphosis is 'undocumented' and therefore cannot be explained; Woolf cannot, at this crucial juncture, fulfil 'the first duty of a biographer, which is to plod, without looking to right or left, in the indelible footprints of truth'. Orlando now reads incessantly. It is not even certain that he is still living in the real world. The 'whole vast accumulation' of his estate turns to mist once he opens a book. Perhaps he has been stolen away by the spirit of literature, where we cannot follow him?

There are many passages in *Eminent Victorians*, by Lytton Strachey, which parallel these techniques – though his Victorians were still a living memory when he biographised them. Here is his portrait of Cardinal Manning, which rejoices in asking questions that suggest how resistant to interpretation – and thus how real – Manning's relations with 'his' century could seem:

In Manning, so it appeared, the Middle Ages lived again. The tall gaunt figure, with the face of smiling asceticism, the robes, and the biretta, as it passed in triumph from High Mass at the Oratory to philanthropic gatherings at Exeter

Hall, from Strike Committees at the Docks to Mayfair drawing-rooms where fashionable ladies knelt to the Prince of the Church, certainly bore witness to a singular condition of affairs. What had happened? Had a dominating character imposed itself upon a hostile environment? Or was the nineteenth century, after all, not so hostile? Was there something in it, scientific and progressive as it was, which went out to welcome the representative of ancient tradition and uncompromising faith? Had it, perhaps, a place in its heart for such as Manning – a soft place, one might almost say? Or, on the other hand, was it he who had been supple and yielding? He who had won by art what he would never have won by force, and who had managed, so to speak, to be one of the leaders of the procession less through merit than through a superior faculty for gliding adroitly to the front rank? And, in any case, by what odd chances, what shifts and struggles, what combinations of circumstance and character, had this old man come to be where he was? Such questions are easier to ask than to answer; but it may be instructive, and even amusing, to look a little more closely into the complexities of so curious a story.

As for Orlando, his later metamorphosis, into a woman, comes as a little explosion of joy. Orlando has been freed from time; now to be free, at last, of (one's) sex! The rest of the biography is a discreet cry of triumph.

When Woolf laid down her pen, towards the end, as the darkness gathered in her study, did she feel that she had at last exorcised the long shadow of her father, the editor of the *Dictionary of National Biography*? 'I have had my vision,' she thought, perhaps, reaching for a cigarette. The frayed sleeve of her cardigan swept away a few strands of tobacco; her hand trembled slightly as she struck a match (was it with desire for Vita? Or was she thinking about dinner? Or was she suppressing the laughter that suddenly – we do not know why – welled up inside her?)

She also wrote other biographies – of Roger Fry, and of Eliza-beth Barrett Browning's dog Flush, for instance (see below). But *Orlando* is generally accounted her best contribution to the genre.

The (Real) Life of Sebastian Knight

The power play between biographer and biographee is more complex than is imagined: each is each other's creature (or even *créature*). This is brought out in many fictional presentations, such as Nabokov's novel *The Real Life of Sebastian Knight*. Knight is a famous English novelist – a nocturnal figure, moving unpredictably around Europe between the wars, suffering the slings and arrows of outrageous fortune with almost saintly forbearance. The author, V, is writing this biography largely as a counter-blast to an earlier one by the misnamed Mr Goodman, Knight's secretary, and a vulgarian. 'In his slapdash and very mis-leading book, Mr Goodman paints in a few ill-chosen sentences a ridiculously wrong picture of Sebastian Knight's childhood. It is one thing to be an author's secretary, it is quite another to set down an author's life [...].' V is particularly scandalised by the way Goodman has 'de-Russified' SK, claiming that the poor boy had been forced to endure a foreign influence quite at odds with 'the rich English strain in his blood'.

Nabokov himself showed a peculiar fascination with the biog-raphical details behind Pushkin's *Eugene Onegin*; and immediately parodied this obsession in *Pale Fire*, where the damage done by the commentator-biographer proves fatal. Charles Kinbote goes a bit too far, despite the homage and affection represented by his scrupulous edition of John Shade's 'Pale Fire', when he claims, in characteristically clumsy syntax (but then English was not his native language):

Let me state that without my notes Shade's text simply has no human reality at all since the human reality of such a poem as his (being too skittish and reticent for an auto-biographical work), with the omission of many pithy lines carelessly rejected by him, has to depend entirely on the reality of the author and his surroundings, attachments and so forth, a reality that only my notes can provide.

Shade himself did not relish being read biographically. But, as Kinbote concludes with grim satisfaction: 'for better or worse, it is the commentator who has the last word'.

Unfortunately, the biography of Sebastian Knight, even as it strives to avoid becoming 'one of those "biographies romancées" which are by far the worst kind of literature yet invented', degenerates into a predictable postmodern exercise in scepticism. V thinks he is visiting his dying brother, but sits by the wrong bed. The 'Russian gentleman', his brother, had died the previous day, as the flustered nurse explains. The last paragraph comes to terms with this disappointment which is also an appointment kept, for V has an epiphany. 'Whatever [Sebastian's] secret was, I have learnt one secret too, and namely: that the soul is but a manner of being – not a constant state – that any soul may be yours, if you find and follow its undulations. [...] try as I may, I cannot get out of my part: Sebastian's mask clings to my face, the likeness will not be washed off. I am Sebastian, or Sebastian is I, or perhaps we both are someone whom neither of us knows.'

This collapse into what Hegel might have called a speculative identity of subject and object is perhaps a little predictable. The biographer need not mirror the biographee, nor are we con-demned to wander in the mazy meanderings of the *imaginaire*. As for the self-reflexive games played by V, how *passés* they now seem, as predictable as the mythological apparatus with which Milton filled his 'Lycidas', nymphs and shepherds 'such as a College easily supplies', as Samuel Johnson sneered. Still, *The Real Life of Sebastian Knight* is a last efflorescence of the long tradition of experimental biographies.

When Andrew Field suggested to Nabokov that he, Field, write the Russian's biography, Vladimir Vladimorovich was hesitant. Maybe if he, the noted lepidopterist, were to write Field's biography at the same time…? Field, with remarkable sangfroid, offered to give Nabokov the contact details of his (Field's) ex-wife. This seems to have embarrassed the uxorious exile. He never wrote a biography of Field (at least, not in so many words).

Life of Betjeman

A biographer can hardly be accused of feeling possessive about her biographee. She has lived with her, often for years; she has read letters and diaries, and has prised out so many secrets; she naturally wants to control the extent to which these intimacies are divulged to an expectant world. Another biographer may be a helpful collaborator, a fellow enthusiast. More often than not, she will be seen as a potential rival. How can the biographee (long since dead, but then again…) allow such a rival to share her favours? Biography is not a science (nor is science): it is a field of desire and jealousy, of tussles for priority, of a delicious agonising over privacies trespassed on and ransacked files. All of this has been explored in many novels, notably A.S. Byatt's *Possession*. Thus it was that, when A.N. Wilson and Bevis Hiller clashed over their respective biographies of John Betjeman, the press could only watch in admiration. In the same way, they remarked, Odysseus and Ajax had struggled over the armour of the dead Achilles.

Life of Ronceraille

In the spring of 1973, the French were shocked to read in their newspapers of the death of promising young French writer Marc

Ronceraille, who had been killed in a solitary mountaineering accident on 18 April on the slopes of his beloved Mont Blanc massif. He had already made a name for himself: he lived up with brio to the image of the sixties French intellectual – an athlete who performed for his country at Olympic level,[20] a playboy who liked his cars and his women to be fast, at home both in the smoky jazz clubs of Saint-Germain-des-Prés and in the rural tranquillity of *la France profonde*. In that world of what Beauvoir called *les belles images* (the same world which Guy Debord analysed as *La société du spectacle*) he made a living from selling images, entering the advertising agency Polypublicité in 1963 (such agencies were in those days more 'bohemian' than they are now); 1968 brought him onto the stage at the Odéon theatre, occupied by students, where he made his intervention '*la Parole fait la fête*' ('Words are partying'). In 1969, he became the lover of the actress Fabienne Corot, and managed the publicity for her new film; but their relationship soon turned stormy. In 1972 he broke up with her. It may have been an attempt to cope with her loss that drove him, the following years, to the mountains, though the rumours of suicide were as speculative as they were painful to his grieving family.

After the usual flurry of respectful obituaries and *hommages*, a few years went by in which Ronceraille's work was gradually absorbed, this time under the sign of mortality, by the French literary establishment. Then, in 1978, the Editions du Seuil celebrated the hundredth number of their series '*Ecrivains de toujours*' ('Writers of All Time') by dedicating it, under the aegis of the writer Claude Bonnefoy, to Ronceraille. The *Ecrivains de toujours* series had a distinguished reputation: it covered a canon of writers, both French and non-French, in short but dense books that at first glance looked somewhat old-fashioned (very much a life-and-works approach, with copious quotations from the author in question, a rich selection of illustrations, opinions of his or her contemporaries and later critics, and so on) but were often cutting-edge in their approach: Charles Mauron psychobiographising Mallarmé, another Bonnefoy (Yves) showing the link between Rimbaud and fundamental ontology and, amusingly, Roland Barthes co-opting himself as a 'writer of all time' in a series of fragments that mingled a first-person confessional and anecdotal approach with a third-person attempt to pre-empt his biographers and critics – he thought that to say 'he' of himself was a way of viewing himself as already a bit dead, or from the standpoint of someone else, or as a character in a novel, etc.

The Claude Bonnefoy compilation was equally experimental. Unlike other volumes in the series, it was a real collective biography, with essays from a variety of writers, all of them espousing different points of view. What they bring out, between them, are the profound contradictions that run through Ronceraille's work. So much of his writing seemed to be earthy or even subterranean. Martial, the hero of his novel *L'architaupe* (the title means, among other things, 'the arch-mole', with wordplays on 'architect' and other *archai* or beginnings-and-foundations), loves digging, excavating, in the garden and the cellar of the *'vieux mas'* where he has sought refuge from the alienation of life in Paris. This seems like an 'absurd therapy' – but not if we remember the 'archaeologies of knowledge' in Foucault, or the 'de-sedimentation of western metaphysics promoted by Heidegger',[21] or Freud's digging through the strata of the psyche. He also wrote a volume of poems called *Sol memorable* ('Memorable soil') which bring out his longing to be 'earthed', his need for roots – together with a propensity for puns that make it impossible to detect what Lacan would call the *'point de capiton'*, or anchoring point. And it is ironic that this delver of depths was also a dedicated mountaineer, addicted to the intoxication of height. His texts explore origins: they are structured by contrasts that a structuralist analysis brings out very clearly (earth/stone versus wetness/liquidity, crack/abyss versus penetration/exploration), but also dwell, in a more Bachelardian and phenomenologico-psychoanalytical way, on the more tropes of generation (cave = womb; earth = memory). Yet it would be simplistic to reduce his enigmatic poems, for example, with their spacings and dislocations, to a mere illustration of a theory. Ronceraille *is* his texts: in an untranslatable pun, he states: '*Les repères conduisent aux repaires*' (roughly: 'surveyors will lead you to lairs'). He is, in the sense of Abraham and Torok, a crypt – a place in which something can be both hidden and, at the same time, exposed.

The French have not always been noted for their biographies; one of the ways in which this one, at least, remains exemplary is its refusal to have the last word. Contributors to the volume quarrel with each other, so that Jean-Fédor Bielanski's mythopoeic, freudianising reading of Ronceraille is quite severely criticised in an essay on *Sol memorable*. And the 'life-and-works' approach allows for a subtle reading of the former *in between the lines* of the latter, a signifier that insists and persists, so that the author *is* a '*jeu de mots*', a game with words. When, in *The Mechanical Imagery of Professor Batave*, the Professor says of his friend Buicmosson: 'His ancestor [*aïeul*] had green blood, fanfares in his eyes, and pianos in his trouser pocket [*gousset*]', the critic Pépin notes: 'Replace the first person of the possessive pronoun for the third, and you will obtain an obvious allusion to the author's genealogy.' Origin is vocation in this *matrix* of writing. The '*Ecrivain de toujours*' that is Marc Ronceraille provides plenty of evidence for a vindication of a biographical approach that has learnt how to handle the instruments of the *Nouvelle critique* with tact and precision. 'In spite of recent elucubrations which tend to turn all books into fragments of a continuous discourse, a literary oeuvre remains inseparable from its author. There is no *Légende des siècles* without Hugo, and no *Comédie humaine* without Balzac.'

Of course, Ronceraille himself had read of the 'death of the author', and never fell for the 'biographical illusion' that was denounced so eloquently by Pierre Bourdieu. He teased his friends and critics: 'The more people talk about me, the less they'll know who the real Ronceraille, the author of *L'Architaupe*, is. So much the better!'

The end of the book raises the question of the attribution of some of Ronceraille's works, and it is true that the lack of a real critical edition has hampered further evaluation. Worse, there are no easily accessible English translations of Ronceraille's work, which is difficult to get hold of even in France. Perhaps he is going through the posthumous slump that affects so many writers in the fickle world of literary celebrity. But the poetry is there, in its enigmatic splendour. Ronceraille's time will come.

Part VI
Celebrities and Other Animals

Life of Queenie (aka Tulip)

J.R. Ackerley wrote about himself and his father, as we have seen. He also wrote about his dog, Queenie, the one great love of a life that, for all his male lovers, he found disappointing. He rebaptised her 'Tulip' and wrote her story in his novel *We Think the World of You* and in the memoir *My Dog Tulip*. He evokes her physical beauty rapturously:

> Her face [...] is long and pointed, basically stone-grey but the snout and lower jaw are jet-black. Jet, too, are the rims of her amber eyes, as though heavily mascara'd, and the tiny mobile eyebrow tufts that are set like accents above them. And in the midst of her forehead is a kind of Indian caste-mark, a black diamond suspended there, like the jewel on the head of Pegasus in Mantegna's *Parnassus*, by a fine dark thread, no more than a pencilled line, which is drawn from it right over her poll midway between the tall ears.

She had been brought up in a working-class family where she was treated badly – cooped up in a backyard, given insufficient exercise and beaten for expressing her dampened high spirits. JRA details her *res gestae*, and devotes bracing and solicitudinous attention to her, in particular her love life, which was even more problematic than his own. When she came on heat, he masturbated her into quiescence. Eventually, even beauty revealed the canker in its bud:

> One day, late in her ninth year – the day, I afterwards understood, on which she would have whelped had a mating taken place – when she was sitting beside me in her armchair, she suddenly raised her hind leg and looked down at herself as if in dismay. A flux of bloody muck was oozing out of her. […] She had gone bad inside. She had a septic womb.

Not many biographies evoke the sting of mortal love more honestly.

Virginia Woolf wrote a biography of Flush, Elizabeth Barret Browning's dog, which is also an exploration of class, sexuality, and illness seen through canine eyes. Though less personal, it is, beneath the whimsy, no less serious than *My Dog Tulip*. And, less falteringly than Edmund Gosse's work, it is written against 'fathers and tyrants', however loved.

Life of Lady Gaga

Helia Phoenix's *Lady Gaga: Just Dance. The Biography* was published in 2010, when its subject (b. 1986) was just twenty-four years old. It is a straightforward piece of work that refreshingly avoids the psychological speculation of so many biographies. From the very first page it shows how Stefani Joanne Angelina Germanotta, later self-styled Lady Gaga (and hereinafter abbreviated to LG), was surrounded by music from her birth: her father would dance around with her as a baby, accompanied by Pink Floyd and Led Zeppelin, the Rolling Stones and Elton John. Phoenix also notes, though without this fact being allowed to cast a shadow over the story, that LG, born in Yonkers, grew up close to the Dakota, outside which John Lennon was shot.

What is significant about the biography is the extent to which it draws both on personal acquaintance with its subject, but also on a full range of media: newspapers, fanzines, websites, liner notes. It is also hospitable to rumour: 'rumour has it' that the TV series *Gossip Girl* was based on the Convent of the Sacred Heart, the exclusive (and expensive – about £23,000 per year) school attended by LG – and the action in the series, with its drink, drugs and promiscuity, 'is rumoured to be all the rage at Manhattan's top private schools'. Cristina Civetta, a fashion designer and alumna of the school, has told the *Daily Mail* that her contemporary there, LG, was 'a straight-A student'. LG herself told the gay magazine *Fab* that what interested her at school was the mixture of girls: some with money, some without; blondes and brunettes; 'artsy girls, stoner girls…' She was not herself a rebel, according to an old friend, but she told *Women's Wear Daily* in 2007 that she was mocked for not fitting in ('What are you, a lesbian?', they would ask: adolescents are obsessed by sexual identity, though most grow out of it), and laughingly told About.com that she would do her hair weirdly or overdo the lipstick, 'or whatever I was doing to get attention'. Other publications consulted by Phoenix include: *Maxim* (where LG stated that she was 'amazed by the level of superfan that Britney [Spears] created' and recalled her 'huge boobs' – she later shed twenty pounds); *New Times* ('My parents […] never hindered my creativity'); *Rolling Stone* ('I wanted to have sex with really hot older men'); *The Guardian* ('my schooling […] gave me discipline, drive'); and *Entertainment Weekly* ('My aesthetic is in so many ways exactly the same as it was when I was younger, I'm just smarter').

Like many biographies, this one is eager to locate the turning points – or, in the case of a celebrity, the Big Break. In LG's case this took place when she was in a New York boutique, singing to herself as she browsed the tutus. A store employee named Evan was taken with her voice and told her to contact his uncle, a voice teacher. This was 'the legendary Don Lawrence', who also had Mick Jagger, Bono, Annie Lennox, and Beyoncé as pupils. LG had already been plonked down in front of a piano by her mother and told she would sit there for an hour every day – whether she actually played the instrument was for her to decide. She did, and aged just thirteen had begun to acquire some sense of a musical tradition: 'I started noticing that the Bach chords are the same chords as in this Mariah Carey record'. The range of her influences grew: Carole King, Patti Smith, Grace Jones, Madonna (of course), David Bowie and Queen. Her stage name 'Gaga' came from her love of Queen (see, or rather hear, their song 'Radio Ga Ga' – which a computer spell-check apparently converted to 'Lady Gaga'). LG hung out at St Jerome's with her boyfriend Lüc Carl, with a small stage for a gogo dancer: Gaga too started to gogo. She took drugs. 'In order to achieve the artistic lifestyle that the likes of Andy Warhol and Mick Jagger had led before her, she used to order a bag of cocaine from a delivery service, do some lines, then work on her hair and make-up for hours. She would wake up in the morning at ten-thirty, do some more lines, write music, then stay up for three days in a creative whirlwind of drugs, drink and music.' Characteristic of the modern celebrity musician is the extent to which the art requires a certain, very definite life: a chemical ascesis, but also the absorption and transmutation of so many different contemporary influences. But her second breakthrough came when she took off her clothes at a gig that was not going well, and quietened the restless NYU students by playing the piano in underwear and fishnet tights. This proved to be a moment of real artistic emancipation, as she told the *Independent*: 'it was a performance art moment there and then… unless you were in the audience in that very spontaneous moment, it doesn't mean anything'.

Her hit single 'Paparazzi' was a critique of fame. Like the reclusive and yet much-photographed and companionable Nobel Laureate Samuel Beckett, or, closer to our own day, Lady Diana, LG has always had an ambivalent relationship with her own notoriety. The shift to fashion marked another stage in her evolving relationship with the goddess *Fama*. She said:

> You have the ability to self-proclaim your own fame. You have the ability to experience and feel a certain amount of self worth that comes from a very vain place, by your choices – your opinions about fashion, about music, about politics, the way you walk down the street, the way that you carry yourself at parties – you can literally choose to have fame.

And: 'Me and my friends just simply declared fame on our own, and we made art and we said, "This is the future" and we dressed in a way that says, "This is fashion".'

The prophecies of Nietzsche and, more ironically, Baudelaire, echoed by Foucault, have come to pass; art – the heroic stylisation of every moment, the metamorphosis of everyone into a dandy, the elevation of the will into a supreme criterion of worth, have come to pass. LG, unlike most of us, does not slob around in a dressing gown or a tracksuit at home. 'Typical daywear for her would be an animal-print bikini, a pink sequined belt, black spandex leggings and Jimmy Choos', notes Phoenix. Oddly, her intense individuality does not protect her from being taken for someone else. She was once confused with Amy Winehouse at Lollapalooza, Chicago.

It is possible to watch Lady Gaga's life being constructed in front of our eyes. As the biography shows, the raw materials for the life will also be the sources for all future 'lives', which may not exist even primarily on paper. Lady Gaga is now diffracted and reassembled through: tweets, blogs, email, etc.; interviews in various media; CDs and DVDs; YouTube and other videos; journalistic media of every kind (fanzines, music mags, style mags). Her life can be reported on instantaneously. At a showing of the 2011 documentary about her, *The Lady Gaga Story: One Sequin at a Time*, some members of the audience tweeted compulsively. LG's life belongs in the shifting sands of the World Wide Web. She renders all paper biographies of her mere stop-gaps: even those that will be written when she is no longer here in person will rely less on paper than on other media. Even the most probing biographer may have access to little more evidence than is already available to all in the public sphere.

(My account may sound sarcastic or negative: it is not. It is fascinating to see what hyperspace will make of biography, when it offers unlimited capacities for archiving practically every moment of one's life, and for offering appraisal of... *the lives of others*.)[22]

Epilogue

Stuart: A Life Backwards, by Alexander Masters, tells the story of Stuart Shorter, a homeless beggar in Cambridge.

Unusually, this is a biography in which the subject is allowed to intervene – so much so that the narrative is the site of a fierce, hectic, often comic struggle between biographer and biographee. Stuart volubly protests at Masters' spin on his life, corrects details, insults him ('middle class scum ponce'), refuses information – but at other times cooperates on Masters' attempts to trace the story of how Stuart has become himself (hence the 'life backwards' – without being overly forensic, the book tries to find out how it all began: Stuart's career as a robber of post offices, a prison rioter, an alcoholic, an addict to a whole pharmacopeia of drugs, a lover of knives and casual violence).

Masters' work shows in an exemplary way how biography is a struggle between the randomness of everyday life, its contingencies, its 'shit happens', its sheer senselessness – and the desire for order, pattern, meaning, explanation. This is *mis en abyme*, as it were, since the struggle between meaning and absurdity, between order and disorder, is what Stuart is himself all about, in the rawest of senses.

Masters writes:

Sometimes Stuart seems like an irritable fisherman. He bobs about, on the disruption of his life, a small, unsteady figure, fishing for order. Then he gets into a rage, 'goes right on one', and it's as if he's taken out the gutting knife and mashed his catch to pulp – every sign of hated, repressive, reminding order is gone again. Because order has also been the abiding malevolent force in Stuart's past – police order, prison order, court order, order in the care homes run by council-sponsored paedophiles: the order of 'the System'.

This tussle between disorder and order occupies a large part of Stuart's time.

Stuart likes 'plots'. These are of a paranoid nature: his girlfriend and the ventilation repairman are out to record his conversations; a visiting city councillor was planting heroin. The biographer too is an object of suspicion. 'I am not writing a book about him, I am eliciting confessions that will be used to justify locking him up for good the next time he finds himself in court.'

Stuart was killed, at the age of thirty-three, when the 11.15 train from London King's Cross to King's Lynn ran over him outside Waterbeach, his home village. The inquest found there was no evidence that he had deliberately walked into the train's path (the angle at which his body was found apparently suggested that this was not a case of suicide: at all events, the jury returned an open verdict).

Sometimes a life is so marginal that the only way it can be reconstructed – the only way it can be surmised that there was ever a human being here – is through the work of forensic laboratories. The techniques used are sometimes similar to those of archaeologists, who attempt to piece together from bits of bone, traces of pigment, mitochondrial DNA, specks of pollen, and tarnished bracelets the lifestyle, and something of the life story, of an individual who may have lived thousands of years ago. These days, forensic sculptors may attempt to recreate a face that has been wiped from history. Frank Bender, one such sculptor, was recently in the news as, in June 2011, aged seventy, he entered a hospice suffering from terminal cancer. As David Stout reported in *The New York Times* of 20 June, Bender has, for decades, 'stared at human skulls, handled them, even boiled scraps of flesh off them'. Then he has fashioned clay busts, hoping to identity 'rotting corpses and skeletons found in woods or alleys or abandoned houses'. Identify: give, at least, a name to that which is no longer there, to re-embody, in a tractable if somewhat fugitive medium, a shape that *was* there. He has also studied photos taken years before of murderers still on the run, then used his imagination to sculpt busts showing how they might look now: a kind of three-dimensional identikit. (Did he imagine how their crimes might have aged them? Did the busts follow the law traced on the picture of Dorian Grey, so that his updating made the faces of these fugitives look even more wicked than the photos from which he was extrapolating them?) 'His work,' says Stout, 'has helped the authorities capture several notorious criminals who may have thought they were safe in their new lives.' It comes as no surprise that Bender's studio in Philadelphia had once been a butcher's shop.

Before being admitted to the hospice, Bender was trying to complete what may be his last case. The decomposed remains of a woman had been found by a deer hunter in woods in the east of Pennsylvania in December 2001. It is not known how she died. The anthropologist, Thomas A. Christ, who examined her remains, thought she could have been between twenty-five and forty years old, probably of European descent – though her molars gave some indications of an African origin. Neither dental records nor DNA were of any avail in the subsequent nationwide computer search. After almost a decade of inconsequential investigations, police called on Bender's expertise. He is greatly esteemed for his ability to scrutinise a face (or what is left of it) in the greatest detail; his measurements of a skull enable him to put flesh on the bone. Maybe, it was suggested, since no family or friends had tried to seek the dead woman, she had been a prostitute or drug addict (the kind of women who often do go missing without trace)? Wrong, Mr Bender said. The extensive dental work, including a root canal and crowns, suggested that she had had resources, sophistication, self-esteem. Maybe, he said, 'she got a divorce, was feeling her oats, wanted to start a new life – and met the wrong guy'. I have no way of knowing how reliable this inference may be, but it is fascinating that, from the woman's teeth, a 'type of person', and even episodes in a rudimentary life story, can be deduced. Bender had left the lips of the bust he had created slightly parted. Why? He said that he didn't know – 'it just works'. (It made the woman look as if she were about to say something.)

Bender's intuition had proved effective before. On one occasion, a young woman's body had been found in a field just behind a high school. For some reason – perhaps simply because she had been a young woman – he imagined her yearning for a better life. When he fashioned her bust, he gave her head an upwards tilt. It was eventually recognised by her grand-aunt: the upward tilt of the head was a trait of the girl's, as evidenced by a photograph. Her murderer eventually handed himself in to the police.

Those who have worked with Bender say that his refusal to use computers, but to rely instead on his art as a sculptor, is justified. He can capture 'personality' where a computer cannot.

The case of the woman found in the woods is still open.[23] Frank Bender, facing death without fear (like many of those who have come face to face – in his case literally and repeatedly – with death), is still able to see his friends from the Vidocq Society, a group of volunteers that he co-founded in 1990 to investigate unsolved crimes. Eugène François Vidocq (1775–1857) was the name of the French criminal who, as a thuggish young man with a flashing rapier, was nicknamed 'le vautrin' ('the wild boar') by his associates. After committing various thefts, he worked as a monster in a fair, a puppeteer, and a soldier. He deserted, and became a man of many pseudonyms (including 'Monsieur Rousseau'). He pretended to be a French aristocrat on the run from the Revolution in order to marry a rich widow (though he decided not to go through with the deception), and lived with the gypsies. He was also in and out of prison, from which he escaped many times, on one occasion disguised as a nun. Facing jail again, after time as a cattle drover, a sailor, an Austrian and a businessman, he decided to give up life on the run, and offered to act as a police spy. His insider knowledge of the criminal world made him an excellent informant, and he eventually rose to become chief of the Paris police. He was crucial in the development of modern forensic methods (such as the use of index cards), and it was said that he had 'a photographic memory', especially for the faces of criminals. He fascinated many of his contemporaries: it was on Vidocq, whom he new personally (and who had his ghost-written *Memoirs* published in 1828),[24] that Balzac modelled the career of his fictional player-of-many-parts and master-of-many-disguises Vautrin, who also rose up through the criminal ranks, via many metamorphoses, to become *chef de la Sûreté*. (There is a sci-fi version of some aspects of this archetypal poacher-turned-gamekeeper, *Vidocq* (2001), starring Gérard Depardieu, who is also something of an actor.)

The title of David Stout's article on Frank Bender is: 'Recomposing Life's Details from Scraps'. It would be a suitable epitaph for biographers.

Notes

1. An essential part of the biography of Christ produced by Pasolini is the soundtrack to his film. This includes 'Sometimes I feel like a Motherless Child', the 'Misa Luba', Webern's 'Passacaglia', and the final chorus ('Wir setzen uns mit Tränen nieder') from the *Matthew Passion*.

2. In the winter of 1941, German troops were approaching Moscow. Stalin ordered the icon to be placed in an aeroplane and flown several times round the capital. Several days later, the Germans began to retreat.

3. See Lily Tuck's biography of Morante, *A Woman of Rome* (2008).

4. There are, of course, quite specific historical references in the Koran – for example, to the Battle of Hunayn (9: 25–26).

5. The second pontiff of that name.

6. This would presumably debar – to take just two examples who happen to be buried in the same cemetery, Père Lachaise in Paris – both Jim Morrison or Allan Kardec (neither of them, I suppose, currently being proposed for canonisation by the Catholic Church). I have witnessed somewhat dubious rituals at the latter, though the inscription on Kardec's tomb is perfectly orthodox, and a nice challenge to any biographer: '*Naitre, mourir, renaître encore et progresser sans cesse, telle est la loi*' ('To be born, to die, to be reborn and to progress ceaselessly, such is the law').

7. A translation of the *Legenda Aurea* was published by Caxton in 1483; it is this which I quote here, with slight modifications.

8. This honour was awarded them by Pope Leo XIII. The publishing house still exists as Burnes & Oates, an imprint of Continuum, publishers of books in a wide range of subjects, including Paolo Freire's *Pedagogy of the Oppressed*.

9. The negative image of a piece of cloth held in Turin Cathedral, in 1898, was to give added momentum to the debate about the relationship between photography (as image and icon, or as piece of scientific evidence, or as easily fakeable medium) and the sacred.

10. Her full name was Gemma Maria Umberta Pia – which seems, fortuitously perhaps, a nice mixture of the secular/*Risorgimento* (there was – as yet – no Saint Gemma, and Umberto I had just been crowned king of Italy) and the pious.

11. Alain Cavalier's 1986 film *Thérèse* was an effective film biography: it starred Catherine Mouchet in the title role. Mouchet found her career somewhat hampered by this early identification with a saint, but she has since played a psychoanalyst, a prostitute, etc. A reviewer for *Time Out*, I think, commented that Thérèse seemed to have been sainted for doing very little. A fair comment, but it perhaps misses the point (Thérèse died at the age of twenty-four, when most biographies would not have a great

number of achievements to record; and sanctity is a balance between the virtues of doing and being, or the active and contemplative lives), but it does indicate the difficulty in writing the biography or, a fortiori, making a biopic of someone whose experience is essentially inner.

12. Jokes about the Italian postal services are customary at this point.

13. Julien Sorel, in Stendhal's *The Red and the Black*, took Napoleon as his role model. Whom did Napoleon take as a role model? Caesar? Alexander? Actually, as important as either of these was Goethe's lachrymose and maundering hero Werther.

14. There is a website devoted to Gemma Galgani: stgemmagalgani.com. At the time of writing, it includes a rather disturbing photograph of Robert Powell.

15. Alternatively, life is always already mythical.

16. *Aeneid*, book VI: 'to spare the subjected, wear down the proud in war'. Not always an apt summary of Roman foreign policy (see below, on Agricola).

17. There are indeed many fine collections of anecdotes about philosophers – in Diogenes Laertius, Simon Critchley, etc. Philosophy is essentially a way of life, as the Pre-Socratics well knew. It is baffling why Heidegger should have been so hostile to biography.

18. These have been especially in making sense of the words of somewhat inarticulate MPs.

19. I discuss the way that life – and 'a life' – cannot just be dragged across linguistic borders, in my study of modern translators, *The King Is Naked* (forthcoming).

20. He is widely said to have reached the finals, but was actually eliminated in the quarter-finals – the error seems to have been due to a journalistic typo.

21. 'De-sedimentation' was a name that Derrida considered adopting for his own approach, before settling on 'deconstruction'.

22. I present other examples of biographies ancient and modern at: http://benequilatuit.blogspot.com.

23. For details, see www.solvethiscoldcase.com.

24. There is a recent biography by James Morton (*The First Detective: The Life and Revolutionary Times of Vidocq*, 2004).

Biographical note

Andrew Brown is a college dropout and freelance translator from the Black Country. His other works include two 'Brief Lives' for Hesperus Press – *Flaubert* (2009) and *Stendhal* (2010) – as well as a series of prose poems in dialect, *Yoe doe arf goo all round the Wrekin*; a short survey of notable fakes, *Playing in Winter's Sun*; and a satirical study of life after Babel, *The King Is Naked* (forthcoming). He is the founder of the underground association RAGOUT (Revolutionary Anarchist Group of Utopian Translators).

HESPERUS PRESS

Hesperus Press is committed to bringing near what is far –
far both in space and time. Works written by the greatest
authors, and unjustly neglected or simply little known in
the English-speaking world, are made accessible through
new translations and a completely fresh editorial approach.
Through these classic works, the reader is introduced to
the greatest writers from all times and all cultures.

For more information on Hesperus Press, please visit our
website: **www.hesperuspress.com**

SELECTED TITLES FROM HESPERUS PRESS

Author	Title	Foreword writer
Pietro Aretino	*The School of Whoredom*	Paul Bailey
Pietro Aretino	*The Secret Life of Nuns*	
Jane Austen	*Lesley Castle*	Zoë Heller
Jane Austen	*Love and Friendship*	Fay Weldon
Honoré de Balzac	*Colonel Chabert*	A.N. Wilson
Charles Baudelaire	*On Wine and Hashish*	Margaret Drabble
Giovanni Boccaccio	*Life of Dante*	A.N. Wilson
Charlotte Brontë	*The Spell*	
Emily Brontë	*Poems of Solitude*	Helen Dunmore
Mikhail Bulgakov	*Fatal Eggs*	Doris Lessing
Mikhail Bulgakov	*The Heart of a Dog*	A.S. Byatt
Giacomo Casanova	*The Duel*	Tim Parks
Miguel de Cervantes	*The Dialogue of the Dogs*	Ben Okri
Geoffrey Chaucer	*The Parliament of Birds*	
Anton Chekhov	*The Story of a Nobody*	Louis de Bernières
Anton Chekhov	*Three Years*	William Fiennes
Wilkie Collins	*The Frozen Deep*	
Joseph Conrad	*Heart of Darkness*	A.N. Wilson
Joseph Conrad	*The Return*	Colm Tóibín
Gabriele D'Annunzio	*The Book of the Virgins*	Tim Parks
Dante Alighieri	*The Divine Comedy: Inferno*	
Dante Alighieri	*New Life*	Louis de Bernières
Daniel Defoe	*The King of Pirates*	Peter Ackroyd
Marquis de Sade	*Incest*	Janet Street-Porter
Charles Dickens	*The Haunted House*	Peter Ackroyd
Charles Dickens	*A House to Let*	
Fyodor Dostoevsky	*The Double*	Jeremy Dyson
Fyodor Dostoevsky	*Poor People*	Charlotte Hobson
Alexandre Dumas	*One Thousand and One Ghosts*	

George Eliot	*Amos Barton*	Matthew Sweet
Henry Fielding	*Jonathan Wild the Great*	Peter Ackroyd
F. Scott Fitzgerald	*The Popular Girl*	Helen Dunmore
Gustave Flaubert	*Memoirs of a Madman*	Germaine Greer
Ugo Foscolo	*Last Letters of Jacopo Ortis*	Valerio Massimo Manfredi
Elizabeth Gaskell	*Lois the Witch*	Jenny Uglow
Théophile Gautier	*The Jinx*	Gilbert Adair
André Gide	*Theseus*	
Johann Wolfgang von Goethe	*The Man of Fifty*	A.S. Byatt
Nikolai Gogol	*The Squabble*	Patrick McCabe
E.T.A. Hoffmann	*Mademoiselle de Scudéri*	Gilbert Adair
Victor Hugo	*The Last Day of a Condemned Man*	Libby Purves
Joris-Karl Huysmans	*With the Flow*	Simon Callow
Henry James	*In the Cage*	Libby Purves
Franz Kafka	*Metamorphosis*	Martin Jarvis
Franz Kafka	*The Trial*	Zadie Smith
John Keats	*Fugitive Poems*	Andrew Motion
Heinrich von Kleist	*The Marquise of O–*	Andrew Miller
Mikhail Lermontov	*A Hero of Our Time*	Doris Lessing
Nikolai Leskov	*Lady Macbeth of Mtsensk*	Gilbert Adair
Carlo Levi	*Words are Stones*	Anita Desai
Xavier de Maistre	*A Journey Around my Room*	Alain de Botton
André Malraux	*The Way of the Kings*	Rachel Seiffert
Katherine Mansfield	*Prelude*	William Boyd
Edgar Lee Masters	*Spoon River Anthology*	Shena Mackay
Guy de Maupassant	*Butterball*	Germaine Greer
Prosper Mérimée	*Carmen*	Philip Pullman
Sir Thomas More	*The History of King Richard III*	Sister Wendy Beckett
Sándor Petőfi	*John the Valiant*	George Szirtes

Francis Petrarch	*My Secret Book*	Germaine Greer
Luigi Pirandello	*Loveless Love*	
Edgar Allan Poe	*Eureka*	Sir Patrick Moore
Alexander Pope	*The Rape of the Lock* and *A Key to the Lock*	Peter Ackroyd
Antoine-François Prévost	*Manon Lescaut*	Germaine Greer
Marcel Proust	*Pleasures and Days*	A.N. Wilson
Alexander Pushkin	*Dubrovsky*	Patrick Neate
Alexander Pushkin	*Ruslan and Lyudmila*	Colm Tóibín
François Rabelais	*Pantagruel*	Paul Bailey
François Rabelais	*Gargantua*	Paul Bailey
Christina Rossetti	*Commonplace*	Andrew Motion
George Sand	*The Devil's Pool*	Victoria Glendinning
Jean-Paul Sartre	*The Wall*	Justin Cartwright
Friedrich von Schiller	*The Ghost-seer*	Martin Jarvis
Mary Shelley	*Transformation*	
Percy Bysshe Shelley	*Zastrozzi*	Germaine Greer
Stendhal	*Memoirs of an Egotist*	Doris Lessing
Robert Louis Stevenson	*Dr Jekyll and Mr Hyde*	Helen Dunmore
Theodor Storm	*The Lake of the Bees*	Alan Sillitoe
Leo Tolstoy	*The Death of Ivan Ilych*	
Leo Tolstoy	*Hadji Murat*	Colm Tóibín
Ivan Turgenev	*Faust*	Simon Callow
Mark Twain	*The Diary of Adam and Eve*	John Updike
Mark Twain	*Tom Sawyer, Detective*	
Oscar Wilde	*The Portrait of Mr W.H.*	Peter Ackroyd
Virginia Woolf	*Carlyle's House and Other Sketches*	Doris Lessing
Virginia Woolf	*Monday or Tuesday*	Scarlett Thomas
Emile Zola	*For a Night of Love*	A.N. Wilson